Life in the Afternoon

Good Ways of Growing Older

Edward Fischer

Paulist Press
New York/Mahwah

Library of Congress Cataloging-in-Publication Data

Fischer, Edward.
    Life in the afternoon.

    1. Aged—Conduct of life.   I. Title.
BJ1691.F57   1987   248.8′5   87-9090
ISBN 0-8091-2892-6 (pbk.)

Published by Paulist Press
997 Macarthur Boulevard
Mahwah, New Jersey 07430

Printed and bound in the
United States of America

Contents

FOR MARY

hers is a blithe spirit

1

Maturing in December

An American woman touring Mexico came upon a boy
selling oranges at mid-morning in a village marketplace.
An orange seemed just the right thing for her parched
throat. To help the boy out she offered to buy the six he
had left, but he would sell only three.

"Why don't you sell me the other three?" she asked.

"What will I do in the afternoon?" he replied.

That boy knows the secret of growing old.

Unless you have something to occupy your time in
the afternoon of life, especially between retirement and
the requiem, boredom may cause you to sit around
straining your ears to catch the first crack of doom. On
her hundredth birthday a woman made the wry observation that many people who want to live forever don't
even know what to do with themselves on a rainy Sunday
afternoon.

Learning to grow old is as much an accomplishment
as learning to play the viola, and both should be started
early. An elderly woman who had worked with old people
for years approached me after I had given a talk to gerontologists and said, "I wish every young person in this
country could hear what you say." She knows that what
you plant in spring you reap in the fall.

In watching some people move from the prime of life

to old age you see them change a great deal outwardly, but stay much the same inside. If anything they become caricatures of their former selves. They continue to march to the drummer which attracted them in youth. By adolescence their disposition was formed, the style of character fixed. In later years the psychic theme may be played in varied ways, but the melody lingers on. As a Jewish saying has it: "What you become accustomed to do in youth, you do in old age."

So much of the inward life shows in old people's faces. I saw two survivors of concentration camps forty years after the trauma—one face was frightening, the other benign. The traumas of life tend to take you in one direction or another.

Voices as well as faces of old people give them away. They do not develop those overnight. If they have been feeling sorry for themselves, and blaming others for their plight, their unhappiness is evident even at a distance.

Everybody wants attention, said an old monk to me in a monastery garden. When I came upon the Trappist raking leaves, a squirrel kept approaching him, frisking about and darting away. "He's trying to get attention," said the monk. "Like everybody else in the world." This reminded me of something an old priest once said: "During creation God made one big mistake: he did not make enough limelight."

My guess is that some old people are so offensive because they are seeking attention. Instead of making themselves feel important by doing something admirable they go ahead and act unpleasant. Like everyone else they have an inner need to do something that gives satisfaction and earns the esteem of others, only they don't know how to go about it.

An English woman who works in a nursing home observed: "If you have been a brave, or clever, or interesting person, you will reflect these assets until you are finished. I have often heard residents say, 'Five years ago I was still at home; I was still doing everything.' But in the same breath they will add, 'Oh well,' and smile."

Those who say, "Oh well," and smile are continuing to mature. Maturing is not an achievement for early years alone, but for all of life. You need to unfold through spring, summer, autumn, and well up into December.

Maturity, unlike gray hair, won't come by merely time passing. It is worked toward, not waited for. No one is ever fully mature, but the difference is vast between those who continue to unfold and those who stop.

Your attitude reveals your maturity. For instance, to keep free of self-pity and bitterness you need to remind yourself that the important thing is not so much what happens to you but how you feel about what happens. It means learning to compensate, putting aside one aspect of life and turning to another still within range.

The route to maturity is through an ever unfolding vocation. In youth and middle years you may have wondered about your vocation, wondered if you are doing what you were meant to do, but if you live to be old you can be sure that is part of the plan or else you would never have made it. No matter how old you get you should still have something to offer the universe, and in that sense old age is a delayed vocation.

On every prominent rocky peak in the Gobi Desert

in Mongolia is a heap of stones, an *obo*, which is both altar and landmark. Each devout person adds a stone in passing, a symbolic act. Everyone needs to add to the sum of experience by living in an admirable way that is, at once, an act of worship and a landmark.

Upon retirement you may get into a rut, one mistaken for a highway until you become aware of the hemmed-in view. When suddenly released from the restraints that go with making a living, you need imagination and discipline to impose on yourself a new outlook and a new set of controls. No matter how much you hated commuting, and the nine to five job, and the boss, those things gave some organization to your life. A life with order in it, even an annoying order, is preferable to chaos.

Women seem to live with old age better than men. When a man retires he suddenly breaks with the pattern, while a housewife never has such a sudden break with her work. The new generation of women, however, with their attention focused on outside careers, may have as much trouble as men making a sudden break when the time comes.

Studies in this matter reveal that the higher the educational level the better retirement is accepted. Imagination and a repertoire of skills help create a satisfying old age. The well-educated tend to keep some type of activity going that has grown from earlier experience and vocation. Theirs may be an easing off, a gentle transition, rather than a sharp break.

In retirement you should reach a point where making full use of your facilities is more rewarding than making money. A new sense of purpose could give such a lift to your life that your delayed vocation brings a greater delight than the one by which you made a living.

A psychologist said: "In retirement you need to face yourself afresh. Have the courage to explore some other aspect of yourself. Try to find something you have left undone, some interest that got covered through the years. Prove to yourself that you still have reserves, mental and physical."

Retirement might be life's strictest judge. It makes you aware of what you are worth to yourself by revealing what you have been becoming all of those years. If you have not become "somebody" you will not accept responsibility for the tenor of your life, but will expect that relatives, or the government, or some organization will shape your life to your liking. What you really need is to admit that you are responsible for your own happiness and misery, that you create your heavens and hells, and are the architect of your fate.

An eighty-two year old Welsh woman said, "Life is so very sweet, isn't it? So very sweet, I think. If you make it miserable and dull, then it is you and not life that is to blame."

Jung warned against trying to live the afternoon of life according to the program of life's morning. "For what was great in the morning," he said, "will be little at evening, and what in the morning was true at evening may have become a lie."

In my life that has been true. In youth I felt a satisfaction as a newspaperman. Today daily journalism would be all wrong for me. This new vocation, writing books, has grown from the old. Whatever comes next will be all right as long as it brings satisfaction, or else life will become a self-inflicted futility.

Without a new vocation you may find yourself surviving rather than living. You may get the feeling that nothing in life requires your presence: The past is congealed, the present dreary, the future limited. So you freeze.

When you come upon someone who hoards life, instead of using it as an investment, you can learn something. Such people serve as examples of how dreary the clutched life can be. When aware of the boredom that smothers them you may be jolted into doing something that you ought to have been doing all along.

Many people find that they cannot endure the retirement they had hoped for—listless leisure, freedom from effort, uninterrupted loafing. They have awaited the unencumbered years, dreaming of a long Indian summer with nothing to do, and suddenly freedom is a burden. Something is needed to give direction to the day.

Some people sense this danger while still working. In the Dressmakers Union several workers applied for a pension and then changed their minds. One explained, "If I don't go on working, what will I do with my time?" Another added, "If I work I'll stay healthy longer—mentally and physically." They sensed that one needs to become old with a purpose, giving each day a shape instead of letting life become an amorphous blur.

You cannot be happy in old age, and grow in maturity, unless you accept your condition and even enjoy the advantages of it. To lead a life of high serenity, surpressing the ego without losing vividness, is an admirable way to age. In his eighty-second year, Bernard Berenson wrote in his journal: "There is a certain sweetness in being what one is now—not reduced but contracted—so appreciative, so enjoying, so grateful for what has been, and for what is now. It means something to rise above aches and pains and inertias, and to glory in the world as displayed to one's experienced senses and ordered mind."

Unless you feel that way, you may be unfair to yourself. Much is written about how unfair society is to the elders, but they are usually more unfair to themselves. Society cannot make you a dignified, interesting person; you must do that for yourself. To live with dignity you will have to live with the grain and not against it. By refusing to accept old age you are going against the grain, denying your mortality, and so getting out of touch with reality.

Worse than denying old age is dramatizing it. As Byron's prisoner of Chillon said, "I learned to love despair." Some elderly cherish ailments, collecting them the way boys collect baseball cards. Looking into a mirror they no longer see a face, but see a condition. Woe unto those who develop the habit of "feeling poorly."

By the time you get old you should have learned to "allow." Young people are not good at that; they want everything right here and now. But as time passes one ought to learn to allow for less resiliency, and for all of those "aches and pains and inertias" of which Berenson spoke.

In working out their destinies the elderly move in various directions and yet they share a common vocation: *All need to give courage to those who are still on the way.*

When around the elderly, young people feel that they are looking at their future selves. If what they see causes discomfort, this leads to fear and fear leads to anger. If you grow old with grace, those who see you are less apt to rebel against their journey into the future.

A young woman wrote: "I am not afraid to grow old. When in college I knew Father Esser. He was still teaching in his seventies and very much alive. I said to myself, if you can be like that, growing old is nothing to fear."

To rise higher than self one needs models. Each old person should be a model to those who will some day face the inconveniences of accumulated years. It is possible to be a model just in passing, a point often made in fiction where one person influenced another through brief encounter.

In Saroyan's play, *The Time of Your Life*, Joe and a woman meet for the first time and speak a few sentences to each other. They feel sure, as does the audience, that they will never meet again. Joe says that they will often think of each other, and the audience believes that each will have some influence on the other's life.

In the motion picture, *Citizen Kane,* an old man says, "Memory is a funny thing. Fifty years ago I was getting off the Staten Island ferry. It was a beautiful summer morning. I saw a young girl standing there. She was carrying a white parasol. I saw her for at most three or four seconds; she never saw me. Yet I suppose a month has not passed in these fifty years that I have not thought of her."

In my own life I am aware of incidental influences. I recall a man in his seventies sitting astride a horse in

Belgium and one in his eighties descending with caution from a bus in Concord, Massachusetts. I saw them at most three or four seconds; they never saw me. That was thirty years ago, and yet I think often of the self-discipline they reflected and make a fresh resolve.

Each old man taught the same lesson: with discipline one grows old with dignity. The lesson was reflected in the lineaments of the face and in the line of the body. Such reflections come not from one big dramatic effort but from dozens of right decisions made each day: the decision to sit up instead of slump, the decision not to have just one more drink, the decision to stop eating before feeling stuffed, the decision to bestir the body instead of lolling about all day. And decisions of the spirit—the desire to keep interested, to shun self-pity, to avoid bitterness. Such daily decisions are more important than your inherited genes when it comes to determining what you will be like late in life.

The danger is that you will excuse your flaws by saying, "Oh well, that's just the way I am!" because you don't want to make an effort. To improve your way of living you need to inconvenience yourself for a time—whether it is to stop smoking, or drinking, or over-eating, or complaining. All stretching brings aches in the beginning and at every age you need to stretch physically and spiritually.

By now it should be clear that in this book I am not going to look at old age either through rose-colored spectacles or through dark glasses. I learned the approach to avoid and the one to take from magazine articles written by two nuns. What a young nun wrote about the elderly was all lilting prose awash with sentimentality, an excess of sentiment. A nun in her seventies responded with observations clear-eyed and sensible. The young nun, like many well-meaning people, does not realize that sentimentality when received can be a crippling inheritance. The old nun respects the elderly but does not glamorize them, knowing that smothering them in sentimentality not only does them no favors but also makes discerning people shudder.

In reading that exchange of articles I decided that the study of old age needs to be a study of the spirit, coming from experience more than from theory or imagination. Right then I resolved never to write a book about aging until after reaching three score years and ten.

So on this my seventy-first birthday I make a beginning.

2

The Feeling of "Rightness"

The elderly, just as the young, need to be alert to the feeling of "rightness."

In Ireland an eighty year old nun told me that as a girl in Cork she had wanted to evade her vocation. When the mission magazine, *The Far East*, arrived each month she tried to ignore it, even going so far as to put it in a table drawer, hoping that out of sight, out of mind. Finally, she gave in and went to the convent, and, in time, served as a nursing sister in China.

Life in China was most harsh. She had to face up to floods, famine, pestilence, Communist soldiers, American bombers, warlords, insects and rodents, but she never felt she had made a mistake. Although life was hard, and she was expelled by the Reds, she always had the satisfaction of knowing she was doing what she was called to do. She was not tempted to say, "Why did I get myself into this mess?"

If the vocation is challenging, trying to shun it is not unusual. But then comes a pressure on the spirit that will not be denied.

Harris L. Wofford, formerly of the law faculty at Notre Dame, fought against the urge to join the Peace Corps. He said in describing the struggle, "I've been in Africa four times this past year. Each time I got there I

felt myself going into high gear. I had the feeling of being
in tune with the world. I kind of resisted the Peace Corps
for a long time because I felt I ought not to try to do something that was so natural for me. But I couldn't hold out
any longer."

When the pressure to join the Peace Corps was
greatest he was working as a special assistant at the White
House. Finally, in a letter to President Kennedy he de-
scribed the inner struggle. Kennedy understood and
Wofford became a special representative for the Peace
Corps in Africa.

When David Schlaver was a student at Notre Dame
he felt he ought to become a member of the Congregation
of Holy Cross. He also kicked against the goad. Years
later, as director of campus ministry, Father Schlaver
said: "It all came to a head one winter day when I felt that
nagging restless feeling. I said to myself, 'If you can't beat
them join them!' So I walked around the lake and up the
steps of Saint Joseph's hall into the vocation office and
signed up."

False values can cause such intuitive nudges to go
unheeded. For example, too much concern for money
might induce a lost vocation. Some people shift jobs
freely if there is an extra dollar in it.

If your vocation is encrusted with money, that is
wonderful. Then you can exclaim, "All of this and money
too!" But if your vocation does not pay well, you are still
stuck with it because to accept a job for the wrong reason
is a form of self-inflicted pain. The pain might be disenchantment, a Faustian sense of emptiness. Worse, it may
lead to all loss of feeling. A psychiatrist said, "When you

continue as a salesman if you are not really a salesman you become deadened after a time."

Not long ago I overheard a young woman say to a man, "You work for a while and the paychecks are nice. But then you say, 'Hey, I've got to do something more!' "

She is working at a job while feeling she ought to be pursuing a vocation. She needs work that has the feeling of "rightness" for her. She is beginning to realize that she must find the particular task that evolves from her uniqueness. If her own life has no meaning, then she will, in time, attribute meaninglessness to life itself.

She is learning that life without significance is painful. Her inner hurts will only heal when she is true to herself, true to her inner calling. If she continues to work without satisfaction she will become impoverished even though the paycheck is impressive.

I hope that she learns quite young that most victories in life are small. She may think that others are doing big things, winning big battles, but that is not so. If she becomes a force for good she will soon know that the only place the grass is greener is inside her own soul.

Since the dissatisfied young woman does not find the "now" acceptable, she may start looking to the past or living in the future, for until she finds her vocation she will not feel satisfaction in the present. Even when her vocation is settled on, it will not stretch toward the horizon in continuous bright sunlight; there will, at times, be uneasy searches into darkness and danger. Even the smoothest route takes wrong turns.

Prudence helps during all of this, but it is hard to be prudent during the dark part of the journey. There is no insurance against precariousness. The dissatisfied young woman ought not to be overwhelmed by the blank spaces because there will always be blanks between her and where she wants to go. She will need to take risks and pray for the courage to overcome fear of failure.

Margaret Mead led a life that had more than its share of jolts. Yet when she neared the end of her seventy-seven years she said something that suggests she had enjoyed the feeling of "rightness."

Someone asked, "What have you wanted to do in life? What, if anything, has stopped you?"

"I have wanted to do what I have done," she replied. "If I were given a choice to live life over again, there is hardly anything I would change. I would make the same choices."

Such feeling must have surged through Red Smith when, shortly before writing his final column at age seventy-six, he said, "I never wanted to be an actor, never wanted to sell insurance, never wanted to drive a truck. All I wanted to do is what I'm doing."

A vocation even carries with it a certain outward grace. Tom Seaver, the pitcher, said something that demonstrates this. After completing a television series about great figures in sports, he was asked if great athletes have something in common. "When they get their environment—Longden on a horse, Laver on a tennis court, Williams in a batting cage—it's the most comfortable thing each of those individuals has ever done. It's the one thread that runs through all of them."

When the awareness rushes over you that you are doing what you were meant to do, it can bring a great lift to the heart. My friend, Father Martin Dobey, experienced that joy one afternoon in Fiji and described it in such significant detail that it is worth repeating.

He had been a missionary in the islands for nearly twenty-eight years on the day he planned a journey by air from Labasa to Suva. When the flight was delayed because of mechanical problems, the priest walked to the tiny terminal. Palms and sugar cane fields surround the airstrip with a backdrop of rugged peaks, the backbone of the island called Vanua Levu.

Father Dobey sat on the ground to read his paperback but could not focus because the heat beat down in the still, humid air. He began to take notice of his fellow passengers. Most were Indians, as was to be expected in a cane-growing area. The women sat there brown-eyed, inscrutable, and still, enveloped in their bright saris. In contrast, the passengers from the other side of the world, while trying to accept the situation, were restless and chatty—they paced up and down, smoked cigarettes, and drank coffee.

One was an Australian employee of the sugar company; there was no mistaking the strong rugged build and the deeply tanned limbs of the field officer. Then there was the New Zealand crop-dusting pilot, who had to get back home that night. A stocky Indian businessman, on his way to a political convention, owned a hotel, a construction company, and a movie theater in Labasa. The tall Indian man with the horn-rimmed glasses must be a lawyer. Who else would be wearing a conservative collar and a tie in this heat?

The Fijian girls laughed and chatted as though the

delay was one great picnic. One of them phoned a friend and for half an hour spoke of holidays, visits, and assorted relatives.

Father Dobey was suddenly struck with the thought: "This is Fiji! Here in this little airport is a microcosm of our young nation, our society. Here in these few square yards we have the variety of races, cultures, and religions that make Fiji so unique and colorful.

"How different from one another—the tribal Fijian, the immigrant Indian tenant farmer, the Bombay businessman, the intelligent Chinese bankers and storekeepers. The Westerners with their pragmatic aggressive know-how, and the half-dozen smaller island races thrown in as a bonus. Here every day John Wesley meets Confucius and the Hindu pundit meets the pope and the prophet."

While waiting there it struck Father Dobey forcibly: "These are the people I am sent to as a priest, bringing something to enrich them and unify their cultures in Christ. I too am being enriched by them if I accept their ancient culture, wisdom, and riches. What a wonderful colorful place to work! Perhaps that is the hundredfold promised the disciple who gives up father and mother, brother and sister, and all things for the sake of the kingdom."

Father Dobey completed his story: "Fortunately, the pilot was a good mechanic. Forty minutes later we were scurrying through the Suva terminal to make up for lost time. But now I felt grateful for that delay—for the interlude in Labasa that made me see so much."

When you do what you are supposed to do you

sometimes feel that you own "the world with a view." Your internal wealth is so great that you would not exchange places with anyone else. If you have this conviction it is unimportant whether your life is judged by others as successful. It is difficult, though, to imagine that even the insensitive will fail to see a light shining from a life fulfilled. If you do what you are supposed to do, you work from love, and that is hard to hide under a bushel.

This is not the kind of talk one hears during seminars for the elderly. I doubt that such words as mystery and intuition are mentioned. Our faith now is in measurable and observable data, something to feed into the computer.

The French speak of *courage de tete*, the boldness to trust your reason, but it takes even more courage to trust your intuitions, and so maybe that is why they are not mentioned.

People who write paperbacks telling how to get ahead in life don't seem to take vocations into consideration. They tell how to get a raise in salary, how to win an argument, and how to be assertive. They specialize in the checklists and the jargon that are repeated over and over on Career Days.

A high school girl in Oklahoma asked Jeane Jordan Kirkpatrick how she had set out to achieve her "lifelong ambition" of representing the United States at the United Nations. Ambassador Kirkpatrick laughed: "If I had had such a goal, I wouldn't have had the foggiest idea of how to go about achieving it. What I've done in my life is to follow my interests."

I am all for plans in life—they are necessary, they are

something of a discipline, and are at their best when accompanied by the nudge of the Spirit. The problem is to keep an openness, a sensitivity, to inner encouragement.

Young people find it hard to accept mystery, especially the mystery of the future. They would like to know exactly what they will be doing five years from now. They find it uncomfortable to think that destiny is worked out in every present moment and that it is a continual search: the present moment is tied to the past and will influence the future.

Old people also find it hard to accept that the present moment is influenced by the past and influences the future. They may want to retire from life and not admit that they need to keep growing.

Father Schlaver has learned that a vocation needs to keep growing. After recalling the twists and turns his life has taken since he went around the lake to join the Congregation of Holy Cross, he said: "What shape ministry will take for me in the years ahead is now a greater mystery than ever."

The beauty of mystery often shows in how people find their direction in life. Some of the most interesting vocations unfold in unusual ways—sometimes through suffering, even tragedy. There is nothing more startling than adventures in grace.

In Fiji I met a leper, Semisi Maya, whose watercolors have made him known internationally. He paints them with terribly twisted hands.

"My sickness I see as a gift of God leading me to my life's work," he said. "If it had not been for my sickness none of these things would have happened."

Jessamyn West suffered from tuberculosis as a girl. She was so bad that they sent her away to die. She used the time given her to develop her skill as a writer. When she reached old age she had a shelf of novels to her credit.

If you read the collected letters of Flannery O'Connor you will be impressed with how well she accepted her affliction. At age twenty-five she took ill with lupus and was on crutches until her death fourteen years later. She said that her illness so narrowed her activities that it gave her time for her real work, her stories and novels.

Peter Levi believes that two events helped him become a poet: the enforced idleness caused by infantile paralysis and the idleness that followed an automobile accident.

Those artists accepted their ailments because they led to their vocations and made them feel of use. Even the simplest of souls needs to feel of some use. For instance, when I was living in Killiney, in Ireland, I walked to Dalkey to get a haircut. While I was in the chair a man brought in three books and handed them to the barber. After the old fellow had left, the barber said, "Each day I have him go to the library to get three books for me. He's illiterate. He picks books by their covers. In a week I get maybe three books I want to read." The barber was doing a fine thing in helping an illiterate old man feel needed.

Feeling needed helps inner balance. Physical balance declines with age but an inner one should improve with time. Even on the right track you might spoil your life by some imbalance. In your vocation, for instance, you could become excessive and earn the title of fanatic.

Physicists believe that the universe is constantly evolving toward symmetry, so it seems only natural that an individual's life, like the universe, ought to evolve toward balance. A life out of balance in early years is called a misspent youth; one that fails to unfold toward symmetry is a misspent old age.

In your aims, at any age, you need good sense. Of all creatures only human beings sometimes try to be become something they are not. A canary never tries to be a chipmunk, but someone with a tin ear may dream of a career in opera. No use trying to become an angel either, because you will never make it. It is enough to become a civilized human being living a life in the spirit of a vocation.

In youth you may overestimate yourself; in old age the tendency is to underestimate. At any age though, you will find some people believing they can do anything and some fearing they can do nothing. Both are wrong; the truth lies somewhere in between. Cardinal Newman was aware of such a weakness and said: "My first disobedience is to be impatient at what I am, and to indulge an ambitious aspiration after what I cannot be."

When all is said and done, though, at rock bottom everyone has the same destiny. An Irish-born bishop, Edward Galvin, used to remind his missionaries in China of this on the days they felt discouraged. When they were really low, he would say: "You are not here to convert China. You are here to do God's will."

No matter where you live or how old you are that last sentence is meant for you. It is humanity's universal vocation. The meaning of life is found solely in it.

But how do you know where you fit in?

3

The "Oughtness" of Life

In County Wicklow, up in Devil's Gap, I used to talk with Peter the blacksmith. He disapproved of work for the sake of work. There must be more to life than that.

Mere busyness annoyed him as much as it did the Irishman whose mother had lived a life filled with fuss and flurry. He said of her, "Mother will have drowned a year ago tomorrow. She must have been around the lake at least a dozen times since then."

"Keep busy" is the admonition given by all who write about old age, but they don't warn against busyness for the sake of busyness. Mere escapist activity lacks satisfaction. You need to do something that gives you a place in the world that pleases you.

When, in retirement, the life that gave you satisfaction is no longer available you must find a new one. Shifting from one thing to another may mean tampering with security, and that takes courage. Yet finding your new vocation may be one of life's greatest satisfactions.

If you have really matured, fun and games and fame and fortune are apt to pall. They may leave you exhausted, disenchanted, and uneasy with yourself and with the world. Life gets its validity from work accomplished, not from diversions. Some diversions are needed to bring refreshment, but only through significant work do you discover what life asks of you. A diet of constant pleasure—the one some people anticipate in retirement—will, in time, be as repugnant as a diet of only chocolate.

You will get bored and bitter unless you find something that gives meaning to life because your need for human dignity will not settle for less. Since mere divertissement and distractions are not enough, a second career will have to grow from your talents, resources, and interests. As said earlier, these vary greatly from person to person.

Deep inside yourself you realize that life is not a span of time to be got through, but a chance to do something worth doing. Your old age will feel like progress only if it is a part of a great evolving, a moving forward in the working out of the Great Script. You are an artist whose work is to create yourself right up to the end. No one has a right to say when that work is done—that's God's privilege.

So in old age you get your last chance to become what you really are, to uncover your deep possibilities. How sad that retirement often leads to a banal life. Age should not be satisfied with mediocrity any more than youth is.

Fear of failure could be a problem. Some people wonder, deep inside, "What if I try and fail!" They think that if they don't try they can't fail, but not trying is a form of failure. Courage shows in many ways and risking failures is one of them.

You need to take some risks, not wild, foolish risks, but enough to keep you from becoming static. You can't reach even partial fulfillment, without making at least a try at it. And, of course, all success is only partial. Your desire for an impossible completeness hints of a life to come.

Since there are no leftovers in the economy of God there must be a reason that you are still around. That reason is not to trivialize time; if you do that, you may become deeply disturbed.

"I have sometimes thought that the way to crush and annihilate a human being completely would be to set him to do an absolutely senseless and useless thing," wrote Dostoevsky in *House of the Dead.* "If, for instance, he were condemned to pour water from one tub to another and back again, or to carry a heap of earth backward and forward, I am convinced that he would either commit suicide within a few days or murder some of his fellow-sufferers in order to suffer death at once and be delivered from his moral torture, shame and degradation."

Saint Paul urged, "Try to discover what the Lord wants of you."

How discover it?

"The kingdom of God is within you," said Christ.

Inside yourself you find your place in the world. You are not only created by a divine force, but have a force within that helps in the continuing creation. To be aware of this takes sensitivity, trust in intuition, and a common sense that is really uncommon.

The second career that you find in old age will be

more important than the first one, if your first was directed toward fame and fortune and the second is concerned with the spirit.

Scholars say that the word "bread" in the Lord's Prayer, "Give us this day our daily bread," means more than it seems. In light of the tradition of the Old Testament, "bread" also means a kind of life-giving wisdom, a sense of purpose, a direction in life. In other words, "Give us this day enough wisdom and purpose and direction to suffice for the hour."

Vocation used to mean leading the life of a religious, but now it takes on a larger meaning with the realization that all work becomes religious when performed for a right reason. The religious life was known as a calling; each way of life is a calling for those meant for it—chemist, farmer, jockey—it all depends on the approach.

No matter how humble the work it can be a destiny. I knew a waiter, a laundress, a policeman, a bus driver and a blacksmith who turned humble jobs into destinies. By the way they approached their work they made me realize that the thing done with love is greater than the work itself. Their high purpose became an act of worship, a way of letting God into the world. It is not so much a matter of working for the result but of working because the movement toward the result has a feeling of "rightness" about it. In this some people take a straight road and some arrive by a circuitous route.

Work is neutral. The way you perform it degrades it to a job or lifts it to a vocation. For example, a woman behind a counter selling socks can make you feel that she is pleased to see you or that you are an annoyance in her life. She sends you on the way feeling up or down.

Your attitude separates job from vocation. A job you might work at for money alone, but a vocation you work at because you feel that this is what you were meant to do. You stand apart from a job, but you dwell in a vocation.

A response to any calling is the self's encounter with an "Other" whether understood in theistic terms or not. Even an atheist is not apt to live an inspired or inspiring life until finding a vocation. Only then does one become completely an individual, wholly a person.

The "voice within" has been noticed by sensitive spirits throughout the ages. The ancient Greeks, for instance, spoke of it as the *daimon* and Christian writers speak of promptings of the Holy Spirit, divine grace, and providence.

The ancient Chinese used the word *yi*, meaning the "oughtness" of life; there are certain things you ought to do. They also used the word *ming*—fate, destiny—which Confucius felt was the will of heaven. When you do what you need to do to become the person you need to be, it is the becoming that is most important. Not to become somebody is sad, indeed.

The Hindus use the word *Swadharma* when speaking of the individual law of development. This also embodies the *yi* and the *ming*.

Socrates referred to "a kind of inner voice" which he first noticed as a child. Although a philosopher, accustomed to using his reason, when the court asked him to decide whether he preferred death or exile, he knew the

decision was too important to leave to his head. He returned to court saying he had chosen to die, and that if
his decisions were wrong his "inner oracle" would have
opposed him.

The Greeks believed that living in harmony with
such inner promptings leads to happiness.

Artists have the sense of being an emanuensis. Mi-
chelangelo spoke of "finding" his figures inside the great
chunk of marble. Faulkner said, "I listen to the voices,
and when I put down what the voices say, it's right."
Mauriac observed, "When I no longer feel I am taking
dictation I stop." Renoir said that life went best for him
when he allowed himself to move with the nudges, "like
a cork on a stream." Whenever he ignored such intuitions
things went wrong.

Those who wrote about the spiritual life were often
haunted by the inner nudges. Monsignor Ronald Knox,
for instance, used a metaphor: "Keep your hand lying
light on the tiller, ready to catch any breath of guidance
that God will send you." He felt that a vocation is not so
much a choosing as a responding.

Karl Rahner believed that the intuitive nudge is a
contact with the supernatural and although the contact
may be scarcely perceptible it is a moment of grace.

Cardinal Newman said, "God created me to do him
some definite service; he has committed some work to me
which he has not committed to another." He was sensitive to the "kindly light" which leads: "He gives, not all
at once, but by measure and season, wisely." The heroine
in one of Newman's novels speaks of the inner voice: "My
nature feels toward it as toward a person. When I obey

it, I feel a satisfaction; when I disobey, a soreness—just like that which I feel in pleasing or offending some revered friend."

Kierkegaard echoes all of this in believing that "at each man's birth there comes into being an eternal vocation for him, expressly for him."

Tolstoy wrote in his notebook: "We possess a single infallible guide and that is the Universal Spirit living in men as a whole, and in each of us, which makes us aspire to what we should aspire. It is the spirit that commands the tree to grow towards the sun, the flower to throw off its seed in autumn, and us to reach outward toward God and by so doing become united to each other."

Aware of this "Infallible guide" reflected in nature, Elisabeth Kübler-Ross wrote in her journal: "How do these geese know when to fly to the sun? Who tells them the seasons?

"How do we, humans, know when it is time to move on? How do we know where to go?

"As with the migrant birds, so surely with us, there is a voice within, if we would listen to it, that tells us so certainly when to go forth into the unknown."

You do not find out what you are supposed to be doing by fretting over it. Some people prefer to stew instead of doing what the moment demands.

Goethe summed it up: "How can we learn to know ourselves? Never by reflection, but by action. Try to do your duty and you will soon find out what you are. But what is your duty? The demands of each day." A vocation is the whole of life, not a few detached hours called a job.

Even when you have found your assignment you

may still not be free to wander about in it undirected. Anton Bruckner was so aware of his responsibility that he said to a friend: "They want me to write differently. I could, too, but I may not. Out of thousands, God in His mercy has chosen me and endowed me with talent, me of all persons. Some day I will have to account to Him. Then how would I stand before our Lord if I followed the others and not Him?"

The "infallible guide" speaks through intuitive feelings. These are not the usual feelings, not the ones described when you say, "I feel tired," or "I feel sad." What's more, the voice comes unbidden, like inspiration, and cannot be demanded as a command performance.

Early in life your push toward a special way of excellence is tentative. It is lacking in childhood when dependency is on outward authority. In adolescence the inner voice is still tentative but strengthens with growing maturity. As Aristotle said of adolescents: "They are changeable and fickle in their desires, which are violent while they last, but are quickly over." The young tend to lead lives that are meandering and full of trivialities up until they find their star to guide on.

The Greeks felt that one begins to know what is right for oneself "when the young man's beard begins to grow." Knowing oneself, that is maturity. For everyone it takes time, and some never achieve it.

A lack of vocation may be more painful in old age than in middle years. When days are full of commotion the problem does not confront you so readily as in retirement when you are finally free from all those wheeling-dealing inanities. In old age you need a religious outlook that does not necessarily come from membership in a particular church, but from a spiritual orientation, an awareness of the inner self, a feeling that the important part of life is beyond the graspable.

If you are graced with such maturity, you develop possibilities and fulfill a purpose. Life takes on an attractive pattern, a wholeness; it is well-defined and yet subtle, and rich without ornateness. The mature awareness that there is something that I alone must do is the awareness of self-worth, knowing that you are somebody, that you have reason to exist. The thing is to bring your promise to the surface, to develop it so that you become yourself, a fulfilled person. It is a marriage of sorts.

The inner voice at any age seems stronger in some people than in others. No doubt some pay more attention to it than others.

In my late teens I began to sense the direction to take, a sense that grew with the years. The more I became aware of personal mortality, of time running out, the more I was apt to listen to the voice within.

Awareness of the providential seems to come quite suddenly and returns in cycles. People mature inside the way they grow old on the outside, by somewhat sudden steps rather than by slow transition. Time and again I have noticed fairly sudden outward changes in people, but the inner changes were, of course, more difficult to perceive. As for my own experience, an inner change comes, followed by a long leveling off, and then comes another change. So a vocation does not arrive full-blown but is an evolving form, akin to biological growth. Now and then a Saint Paul is struck down on the road to Damascus, but don't plan on such a dramatic call.

When you momentarily see what direction your life should take, your consciousness is higher than its usual level. Then trust what you feel. Don't search for a guru. Don't check to find out if anyone else sees your vision. Learn to respect the intuitive aspect of yourself.

Of course you must then go through the process of setting goals, taking those interminable small steps toward fulfillment. This calls for self-discipline. Some people fail to find fulfillment for lack of self-discipline, the most usual cause for a missed vocation. Dame Edith Evans said, "The word *amateur* may come from the word love, but the professional makes the final sacrifices." Those of us in teaching know students unwilling to make the needed sacrifices. They may feel the urge toward some walk of life that requires much schooling but drop out, reluctant to face the prolonged effort. Chances are they will get entangled in trifles and will drift from job to job like a soul seeking rest.

In failing to cooperate with what your heart tells you, you miss the path you were meant to take. Perhaps through lack of courage you flinch, or you want to play things safe, or lead a cozy life. Often money intrudes: How much is there in it for me? Some people are afraid of the inner push because it offers nothing to grasp; they need to cling to something material.

In writing about this, Simone Weil said: "I saw the carrying out of a vocation different from the actions dictated by reason or inclination in that it was due to an impulse of an essentially and manifestly different order; and not to follow such an impulse when it made itself felt, even if it demanded impossibilities, seemed to me the greatest of all ills."

I don't want to sound as though finding your calling will make life trouble-free. There are enough flaws in the human condition to guarantee you a share of the sadness.

Every path has obstacles and seeming impossibilities, but in following the right one you work through rough spots without feeling that life is absurd. Life makes sense if you explore your own limits in a way that is best for you. In manifesting your best self you lift the level of life not only for yourself, but for those near you, and for the world.

An open-mindedness to God's will and a willingness to be led are gifts worth praying for. If there is no such openness, then praying for divine guidance is a hollow exercise.

A sense of freedom comes if you give yourself to your vocation and do not try to manipulate it. This is different from the way the compulsive careerist operates, attacking each job with a great sense of selfishness.

Surrender to inner promptings and don't try to dictate to them. Even after you say "yes" with decision, which is the best way, there will still be dark days, but you will feel true to yourself. No matter how difficult the work, if it comes from inner promptings you will not see it as "labor," but will look forward to getting on with it.

One of the great sadnesses in living life as a job is that it often brings a taste of ashes. If you fail to follow the promptings, life feels empty and you begin ranging widely. So in the words of Pindar, "Become what you are."

Any honest work can be a vocation providing it is meant for you. It is a blending of love and work that counts. No matter how humble the task a responsibility comes with it; to play your part in the providential with fullness of spirit is a tremendous demand.

If what you do is in harmony with your inner promptings, you will know happiness. As said earlier, this does not mean that your life will be free of ills— friends will die and accidents will happen—but you will not feel lost in a void, the most destructive kind of unhappiness.

Following your own star sounds selfish, but in the long run it is best for everybody. People who do what they are supposed to be doing are not destructive. Somehow they make all of life a little more alive with a radiating wholeheartedness that is good for everybody. Around such people we feel at our best.

Goodness, kindness, thoughtfulness—virtues that everyone applauds—do not exist except when brought to life by some action. To retire to inaction means withdrawing all effort that might cause good things to happen in the world. Soon life will lack meaning.

Anguish comes from feeling that life lacks meaning. The soul that has not found the right journey suffers a spiritual dizziness. Fears, tensions and anxieties take over. Sticking to the main road of your journey all the time may be a little dull; exploring bypaths could add zest, but only if your heart tells you to.

Might not your intuitions deceive you? Those who

have written on the subject admit that inner guidance requires courage, and some humility, and a willingness to bow low. The ultimate conceit is to believe you are free from illusion. Your convictions are always somewhat blurred by blindness and self-distortion. At best things are seen "through a glass darkly."

So some humility is needed. In an old Hasidic tale someone asks, "Rabbi, why do not people hear the voice of God anymore?" The rabbi answers, "Nowadays, no one will stoop so low." Submissiveness is necessary; the way is lighted by grace, and not by an act of will. You ought not to demand a life that suits you, but instead search for it. It is a matter of losing oneself in order to find oneself. With any vocation comes some mystery that takes some humility to accept. By what secret stairway God comes into your life is not always known.

There is also the problem of balance: how much to trust intuitions and how much to fear the inherent weakness in any decision a human being makes? Often the intuitions are ignored because they lack the clean-cut edge of logic and the apparent sureness of scientific proof. If disregarded they may grow weaker, and finally you are left with arid rationalism. A gray fate awaits anybody who thinks that life can be lived out of the head only.

When a seminarian asked his spiritual director how he could test his vocation, the old man said: "Just remember that you won't be able to test it fully until the day you die. It's a day-to-day thing." He went on to say that you don't dare separate a vocation, with its twists and turns and burrs and briars, from the daily act of growth. Once you consider a vocation full-blown it turns artificial.

It can only take on a marvelous shape under the pressure of significant work.

An orderly life, more than anything else, sensitizes your intuitions and makes them trustworthy. When Santayana was in the nursing home operated by the Blue Sisters in Rome, a young American came to visit him. The philosopher said that the young man might stay at the home but would have to be in by nine each night because at that hour the iron gates are locked. Santayana said: "A session of monastic life might deepen your intuition." Although he smiled as he said it, he was making a serious point. Calm and quiet help you find your direction in life.

Anyone ignoring his life's directions is not apt to show magnanimity, the fullness of heart that lifts life and gives significance to work. Magnanimity has become so scarce that when people in service wait on you with a generous gesture you are aware of the rarity of it.

If you don't respect your inner imperative, you may, in time, despair. Only by respecting your calling and taking charge of your life do you become your best. Then you are uplifted and so are the people around you, and also the world.

So when the Chinese philosophers, long before the Christian era, spoke of *yi*, the oughtness of life, and *ming*, the transcendent destiny, they were giving advice to all ages. By all ages I mean the long stretch of eons and also the relatively short years of youth, middle-age, and senescence. Of the seventy-seven billion human beings who have walked this earth, all needed to be sensitive to the nudge, and then go ahead and do what they were supposed to do.

4

Crowding Out Loneliness

A woman in her seventies complained: "They say these are the golden years, but you can't prove it by me." Her hurt was not caused by an outward poverty but by an inward lack called loneliness. She had nothing to give direction to her day, nothing to give a shape to her existence. To be restored to the flow of life she needed something satisfying in her world.

Many old people feel as she does. While experiencing seismic upheavals in the soul, revealing dark strata long inaccessible, they want to cry out as did Hamlet:

O God, O God!
How weary, stale, flat and unprofitable
Seem to me all the uses of this world!

The French existentialists specialized in such despair. Cynicism was to them what soybeans are to us, a national export. Such pessimism is defeating; there is no value in it, especially not in the declining years. Pope John XXIII said that pessimists prepare themselves "for a dry and unhappy old age."

So many people prefer pessimistic news that the mass media feature the horrors of the world. Unhappy souls concentrate on problems rather than on favorable things, not seeming to realize that it is healthier to focus on what is right with their lives rather than on what is wrong.

Such despair is extremely destructive. In the United States 39 out of every 100,000 men between the ages of forty-five and sixty-five commit suicide. The rate increases until 60 out of every 100,000 kill themselves in their late seventies.

I am not trying to further the good feeling promoted by sentimentalists. For instance the sign, KEEP SMIL-ING, is as annoying to me as the one that admonishes, THINK. Any smile or thought resulting from such signs is artificial. Real smiles come from a satisfaction that is not chased after and captured but is a by-product of life well lived.

Darwin spoke of the survival of the fittest in a biological sense; there is also a spiritual survival of the fittest. People who care for the elderly notice that the strong of body are not always strong of spirit. The crowning glory is not a vigorous body but an indomitable soul.

Growth is from physical to spiritual. Olympic athletes are not much given to contemplation, and octogenarians are not winning gold medals. In youth, growth is mostly toward bodily maturity, but in old age, if there is any growth at all, it is toward spiritual fulfillment.

Fulfillment is found in faith, a deep sensing that everything will turn out all right. A Hungarian physician, imprisoned for three years in Siberia, said that what helped him survive the painful experience was faith in God.

Since the health of the spirit has an influence on

loneliness I mention it here, but problems of the spirit, especially in old age, are of such magnitude that they deserve a chapter of their own. In due course I will get to that.

Self-centeredness brings on loneliness as much as anything. Some people are so self-centered that they make a perpetual claim to the status of victim, collecting "injustices" the way hypochondriacs collect ailments. The world is supposed to devote its full time to making them happy. They are so devoted to the negative that when they are gathered with others they use the occasion for complaining.

When you step inside the home of such a complainer you are overwhelmed by the feeling that here is a house haunted by unhappiness—it reeks of foreboding. You realize that maybe you owe it to others to be happy, for happiness purifies the air and sweetens the place. Melancholy is a form of pollution.

The complainer goes through life waiting for the Furies to announce themselves, expecting the worst, maybe even hoping for it. Since people avoid such melancholy ones, it increases their isolation. So those who most need love seem most adept at warding it off. When speaking of such an unendearing fellow, an old Irishman said, "When he dies there will be many a dry eye."

A woman in a nursing home showed the kind of attitude that defeats loneliness. She began a poem:

> I don't mind getting older
> I accept it as I do the moon and the stars and the universe.

And she ended with:

I owe life; it doesn't owe me a thing.

Someone asked Louie Armstrong, "What was the best period?"

"All of 'em," he answered.

Long before the woman in the nursing home and Louie Armstrong said yes to life, a Roman emperor, Marcus Aurelius wrote in his *Meditations:* "What is peculiar to the good man is to be pleased and content with what happens and with the thread which is spun for him."

People who want pity tend to put the blame for their loneliness on someone else. A woman whose husband was transferred from Minneapolis to St. Louis said, "I hate St. Louis! All my friends are in Minneapolis." At the same time there was probably a woman in Minneapolis blaming that city because all her friends were in St. Louis. The flaw is not in the surroundings but in the self, to paraphrase Shakespeare.

Loneliness is not necessarily averted by joining a group. Many people in groups are being lonely together instead of being lonely apart. Bars, for instance, attract the forlorn who hope to escape emptiness, but all they really escape is aloneness. Companionship that requires the stimulus of Scotch is too superficial to heal deep down where desolation hides.

Anyone who wishes to attract others needs to be on good terms with manners and courtesy, two graces required of the elderly more than of youth. If the young are abrasive it may have something to do with "unfinishedness," but an abrasive old person is just plain loutish. In old age you need to examine your own faults with at least as much enthusiasm as you expend on deploring the shortcomings in others. In that way you won't drive too many people from you. One of the hardest things to accept is the fact that "the fleas come with the dog." Friends and relatives will all have "fleas" that you wish they did not; you need to disregard such irritations as the field of those you are close to narrows with the years.

We tend to think that we communicate with words alone, but we say things in many ways—how we dress, how we talk, the expression on our faces, our posture, the spirit that we exude, the manner in which we take care of our belongings, and on and on. We are saying things to the world even when silent. We create an environment, and every environment communicates. We lift life or lower it for all who come near us.

When I was a young teacher, I wore a hat that was quite disheveled. An older professor suggested that I send it into retirement, for the sake of those who have to look at me. He explained that if you own a piece of property, you should keep it up, if not for your own sake, at least for that of the neighbors. They have to live with it, too. "You are somebody else's environment," he said.

As you grow older, you may care less about personal appearance and congratulate yourself on your waning vanity. But still you need to show concern for how you look out of consideration for those around you. Keeping up your appearance is an aspect of charity, one more way of being thoughtful of others. A psychologist said that you ought to watch out for the spots on your vest, because

sloppiness is often the first sign of a deteriorating personality. When you dress slovenly you soon begin to feel
slovenly.

If you make yourself look fit, you tend to feel fit. A
man with a fresh shave, a haircut, a pressed suit, and a
shine on his shoes will feel more up, more kindly toward
the world, than when he is unkempt.

People who say, "At my age it's ridiculous to care
about my looks," might be saying, in effect, "I'm too lazy
to make the effort."

In growing old, the problem is to develop a patina
rather than a tarnish. To be able to wear with grace the
patina of antiquity, that's the thing.

Ruins can be more beautiful than new buildings.
That is more often true with architecture than with the
human structure. Old age can bring out the beauty of
your whole being, but you have to work at it. When a
woman complimented Alexandre Dumas on the way he
had grown old so gracefully he replied, "Madame, I give
all my time to it."

Don't think you are trying to bring back youth and
beauty—that's silly. You are striving for grace, charm,
mellowness—and a part of that comes with careful
grooming.

Some thirty years ago Michel Leiris, the French an-
thropologist, argued that facial expression should come
under the heading of "behavior" rather than "physique."
When an elderly person has an admirable face it developed from attitudes dating back to youth. Sometimes a
young woman with the wonderfully sculpted face that
God gave her spoils it with a surly spirit. At sixty she will

reflect all the charm of a condor. Everything, for good or ill, starts young.

When the elderly complain that nobody comes to see them, it is often evident at a glance why no one does. People don't want to visit slovenly people any more than they want to visit a slovenly house. Your inner self is reflected in the outer self and in the milieu you create. As the old professor observed, "You are somebody else's environment." Good hygiene, good grooming and good outlook are all reflections of manners and courtesy, a part of civility. Everyone can be attractive in some way. Attractiveness is largely interior. You have met attractive people who could never win a beauty contest; their attractiveness is of the spirit.

Courtesy also requires that you be a good listener. Anyone who knows how to listen is less apt to be lonely than someone dedicated to monologue, a deadly form of communication. Father Frederick Faber said that there is a grace of "kind listening" as well as a grace of "kind speaking."

Some people listen with their eyes a thousand miles away. Some are aggressive listeners, frequently interrupting to disagree. Then there is the listener who shows such determined attention that you feel uneasy. Most usual is the one who uses whatever is said to remind him of something similar that happened to him. Listening kindly is harder than speaking kindly.

Silence can be the deepest form of communication. Psychologists are always speaking of the need to communicate, meaning talk, talk, talk. They realize that communication through silence is for relatively few people.

If you go to the other extreme, though, needing always to be near someone, always talking, your sense of security is not brimming over.

Expressing gratitude is also a part of courtesy. There must be more gratitude in the world than is expressed; of the ten lepers that Christ cured, only one said thanks. Surely the others were also grateful, but did not get around to saying so. The one who said thanks must have had the least lonely old age.

Marriage in late life can be an escape from loneliness, if the man and woman have more to share than mutual aloneness. I heard an elderly widow say on television that she would like a husband to put her up in an apartment, pay all of her bills, and take an apartment of his own near enough so that he could come around when she wanted him to take her someplace. If a woman is looking only for an escort and a man only for a housekeeper, they are in for even more loneliness than they had experienced. In a late marriage both are set in their ways and will have to be capable of reshaping their lives and making adjustments. They will need mutual affection, like interests, and similar values to survive the rough seas ahead.

Some aloneness can be a healthy thing, but the tempo of the twentieth century does not allow for much of it. Aloneness is needed if you want to grow in awareness, for it is difficult to find the substance of thought in the midst of hoopla. If you can't escape the hoopla all you can do is to use it as the basis for meditation.

The most persistent lie is that money is the answer to everything, even to loneliness. Various fundings are supposed to be the keys that unlock the gates of bliss.

That real riches are spiritual rather than material is an idea unpopular in our time. Money has its place so long as it is not over-rated. Cicero said that in extreme poverty even a wise man would find old age intolerable, but added that even in the midst of plenty foolish men find old age burdensome.

Everybody's real needs are few; the wants might be inexhaustible. The immature elderly are especially acquisitive. They fight loneliness by grasping—more objects, more money; some even grasp at more food, out of hunger of the spirit, and grow overweight.

A mature person sees through all of the getting and spending and finds that serenity lies in the other direction. A frugal comfort, isolated from a desire for things, has advantages.

"One of the many pleasures of old age is giving things up," wrote Malcolm Muggeridge. He realized that some of the remaining time is well spent in clearing life of its accretions. The good life, he learned, is not accumulating more but wanting less. Anyone who possesses things but is not possessed by them will not have trouble giving them up.

Avarice is always unpleasant to come upon, especially in the elderly. They should know better. How absurd to keep clutching at things so near the end of the journey!

Loneliness cannot be wished away; to get rid of it you need to crowd it out. Without an abiding purpose dry-rot sets in. Until your shadow blends into the shadow of death, you need to feel that you are on the road to fulfillment.

And so we return to the subject of vocation. You find the right road through what Kant called "the small voice of the heart within." Jung spoke of it as an "inner voice" which directed his life.

In a television documentary about a monastery, one of the monks said: "It is a mystery as much to ourselves as to others; it is something we know we *have* to do." They know that if they kick against the goad everything will go haywire in their lives because the transforming force, usually gentle, is not always so. In the *Paradiso*, Dante cries: "In Thy will is our peace."

When you do something because you feel the nudge, the secular answer is that you do it for psychological reasons. That is true. The Almighty created the psyche and does not hesitate to use it.

Things we find painful, such as loneliness, may in the long run be good for us. Many rough roads lead to fulfillment—for instance, that of the bedridden racked by pain. In the age of activists, the bedridden might be made to feel inadequate and alone. Yet suffering is a form of activity. If seen as a vocation, and accepted as such, suffering brings more nobility than all the confrontations of the activists.

To bear affliction with stoicism could cause spiritual sclerosis, a hardening of the heart, but accepting it in the proper spirit leads in the direction of sanctity. A woman who had known an abundance of troubles did not lash out, but said: "God does not make mistakes."

Afflictions deprive, but do not necessarily diminish. A man with cancer, for instance, found fulfillment when he was able to do more than doctors or ministers for the spiritual life of other patients.

Human beings do not look so much for pleasure as they do for meaning, according to Dr. Viktor Frankl. They will even accept suffering, he said, if they see it has meaning in their lives. Meaning and loneliness are not to be found together.

The need to be loved is a basic human need. When you feel cut off and unneeded you feel empty. As long as you are needed you are not apt to feel lonely. So the answer is: Be of some value to others.

A great life, like a great poem, continues to grow in meaning. When meaning is missing there comes a death before death. Some people, not just old ones, die long before their official demise, and since such is not recognized by law, burial must be deferred.

An advertisement in London for a certain shoe polish shows an old but beautifully preserved pair of shoes with the caption: "They are well worn but they have worn well." This describes old people who wage a somewhat successful battle against loneliness. The victories are only temporary, of course: God does not give courage today for tomorrow's battles; tomorrow the lonely will have to pray for courage all over again.

5

A Winter Unseasonably Mild

On this blue planet, whirling in a corner of the solar system, only human beings need to worry about getting design into their lives. There is no need to arrange for a migration of swallows, or put pattern into a galaxy, or adjust the ebb and flow of tides. People alone are capable of chaos.

In growing old you get one last chance to create a design for yourself. In childhood life seemed a collection of experiences rattling around without meaning; in youth, and even in middle years, you could not see the pattern until enough experiences began fitting together to make pictures.

In old age it is possible to see that design can prevail and that caprice plays a lesser role in life than you had thought. If you sense some cohesion in creation, especially in yourself, it brings the gift of serenity, and then your winter days may be unseasonably mild.

Once you sense some wholeness you catch a glimpse of grandeur. Until then you are like someone with nose pressed against the door of the cathedral of Chartres. You miss seeing the awesome design.

Looking for design is a step toward mysticism. Pierre Teilhard de Chardin said that mysticism is the great science and the great art because it is "capable of synthesising the riches accumulated by other forms of human activity." Long ago Heraclitus observed that the failure to sense that everything adds up, that all things are one, is at the root of all evil. So creating a design in your own life, making things add up, is no trivial matter.

A work of art in which everything works together brings an aesthetic experience, a thrill of the spirit that comes when in the presence of some great "rightness." You would not be thrilled by design in art if none were in creation. Everything from the Milky Way to the molecules in your body are of startling patterns, and so it comes natural to be hungry for such.

In old age it is fitting that your life, like a symphony, move toward a finale with a sense of right ending. To impose such a pattern is not done once and for all but is a day-to-day effort.

Everyone has the assignment to turn life into a work of art. Not to do so can be tragic. People talented at putting words on paper or paint on canvas but not at imposing design on their own lives sometimes die by their own hands. It is easier to learn a technique—handling an art form, a science, a language—than learning to create a well-designed life. Technique might be grasped by dogged attention but a unified and varied life with harmony and balance in it comes from a well-formed character. It is true that your character is your fate.

Ideas about the well-lived life have come down through the centuries. Cultured Chinese in the ancient world made some observations that now sound quaint:

If your attitude toward fame and fortune is cool and remote, if you can take them lightly, you are wealthy and wise.

Among the best things in life are books in your study and flowers well-arranged in a vase.

You are rich if you have read the classics and find yourself at home among the rocks, trees, and springs.

If you have "seen through life," you are not too ambitious and are able to put up with disadvantages and obscurity.

This way of looking at life may sound dated, but the Chinese, Greeks and other thoughtful peoples all agreed on one thing: the centrifugal life, one that flies off in all directions, does not satisfy. It merely distracts.

Old-fashioned spiritual directors realized the need for design of the inner self. They recommended reflection and examination of conscience, efforts that would be a waste of time if you were programmed in an unyielding way.

Life seemed terribly unyielding when Darwin explained how determined you are biologically and Marx said you are determined sociologically, and Freud, psychologically. So the tendency was to say that you'll just have to ride it out. Recently the idea has returned that one ought not to blame parents, or race, or social background, but go ahead and give life a direction worth taking.

If you believe that the Almighty did not create the universe in all its completeness but that creativity continues, then you realize that you are a part of the unfolding. To see creativity worked out in each day brings an awareness of the Providential, a more lively way of looking at life than seeing God as setting billions of tops in motion and then turning attention elsewhere. When aware of an unfurling, a "going on" in the world, you remain a part of this dynamic, and enjoy a freshness long after the freshness of youth fades.

Just as no two thumbprints are identical, no lives are written in duplicate. You will have to work out a design for each stage of life and cannot copy the answers from someone else. It has to be something that feels "right" to you. The Scriptures speak of a *kairos*, a time that is just right for something. For a well-lived life it is important to sense what is fitting for the present and to act on it.

The pattern of life in retirement might follow directly from your life's work, as it does for the retired accountant who visits small churches to help with their financial reports, and the elderly executive who advises people starting a small business, and the old priests and nuns who visit nursing homes.

Or the delayed vocation might be so different from your life's work that you will have to prepare for it, as do volunteers who conduct tours for children in museums, art galleries and zoos, and those who visit the housebound to help with tax forms and other matters. They do not get paid for this work, but if it brings satisfaction they are rich even in a low tax bracket.

Your newly designed life will need unity, just the way a unifying motif, or theme, is used in writing, composing, building, and in other creative work. Unity takes bits and pieces and gives them coherence, helps them add up to something, and brings order out of chaos.

A unifying force comes from having a dominant direction—call it a vocation—in your life. Some men look forward to a direction that will not hold up. For instance, one said that he will give his time in retirement to making renovations around the house, but chances are he cannot repaint the upstairs or build shelves in the basement on and on without feeling that he ought to turn to something else. The same with golf, bridge, and travel, short-term distractions that might not bring lasting satisfaction.

To avoid dullness the theme of your life needs variety just as variety is used in a work of art. For instance, the unifying motif in Gothic architecture is the pointed arch presented in windows and arches of varied sizes that shift and change in appearance when seen from different angles as one moves through Gothic space.

In the new-found leisure of retirement you need such variety. By leisure I don't mean idleness, or a pursuit of trivialities, but unpressured satisfying work freely chosen—a delayed vocation.

The transition to senescence is the coming of a new season and as with every season you need to live in harmony with it. All aspects of your life should be in proper proportion. In improving proportion you may learn to do without things and come to enjoy the freedom of traveling light. Stepping clear of the clutter you "find" yourself. In the deprivations of old age you may feel that frugal comfort has advantages.

The winter of life is enriched if you are capable of enjoying *les petites bonheurs*, but you may miss those small happinesses, and keep grasping, if you have been grasping all along. As the Chinese proverb has it: "It is easier to fill the valley than to satisfy human greed."

Balance is another characteristic of good design. The ancient Greeks said that the hardest thing for a human being to achieve is a balanced life. To be in equilibrium means giving the various aspects of life the attention they are due. The tendency is to give trifles more care than they are worth.

A lack of balance can show in a million ways. If, for instance, you expect paradise on earth, or perfection in others, you will suffer a bad case of bitterness because of an unbalanced approach to reality.

In retirement the relationship between husband and wife may waver in the balance. How much they should see of each other becomes a problem. A wife quipped: "I married him for better or for worse but not for lunch." A gerontologist advised a new retiree: "Don't inflict your perpetual presence on your wife."

A balance between mind and body is a problem at any age. It is the mark of an uninteresting person to give all attention to things of the body—eating, drinking, playing. A television documentary told of old people in St. Petersburg, Florida, who are fanatical about shuffleboard, playing morning, noon and night. That is better than a lack of all interest, but still it is dedicating the little remaining time and energy to trivialities. Old age might better give more attention to mind and spirit.

Old age, sustained by "the long view," should reach a balance more readily than youth. Stendhal observed that knowledge of life prevents one "from becoming passionately concerned, from behaving madly over nothing." Such a sense of proportion helps in accepting the thefts of time: one year time steals a dear friend, the next some lower teeth, and the following, a driver's license. Time steals from everyone and is not just picking on you.

Such thefts are unacceptable to the grasping, to those filled with the unsurrendered things of the soul, and so they tend to harp on the trivial. The elderly who can accept such losses bring with them the infection of good courage and even that of happiness. They are more than configurations of tormented atoms. To be able to lack things gracefully—that is a prayer worth saying.

"Teach us to care and not to care" is another prayer worth saying. That haunting sentence is from T.S. Eliot's poem, "Ash Wednesday." Unless you find such a balance of caring you add to your own burdens and to those of others.

Saint Augustine showed good sense in this when he said: "Do everything as though it were the most important act in the world, but also as though you are going to die the next minute and it didn't make any difference."

Eliot was aware of the problem of balance facing those who work creatively. While it takes a tremendous amount of caring to compose a symphony, write a book, or carve a statue, there is a need to hold the work lightly, realizing that in creating anything you are playing God, and that such an effort when compared with God's creation is even less than picayune.

Creative work deserves some caring because at its best it is striving for something good. As an attempt to bring a kind of truth, a "rightness," into the world, creativity is a moral act. Living a moral life is, in turn, a creative activity. A well-lived life is a work of art.

Even morality can get out of balance. When focused on too fiercely it causes fanaticism. The old-fashioned virtues go flat and stale when harped on in an over-zealous way. Thoreau had this in mind when he said: "If I knew for certain that a man was coming to my house with the conscious design of doing me good, I should run for my life."

Like everyone else, T.S. Eliot had a problem of keeping his balance. For one thing he had such a strong nostalgia for the past that he was disillusioned with the present. He told a friend that "The Waste Land" was a "grouse against life."

Such imbalance is very usual. An old lady in Boston said, "No doubt about it, the modern thunderstorm no longer clears the air." In poking fun at such an attitude, someone scribbled on a wall: "Nostalgia is not what it used to be." And yet a film narrator put his finger on some truth when he says at the start of *The Go Between*, "The past is a foreign country; they do things differently there."

Homesickness for the past and excessive disillusionment with the present can throw you out of balance when looking into the future. Such imbalance, common among the elderly, has been usual through all of recorded time.

Nearly five thousand years ago an Assyrian chipped into a stone tablet: "Our earth is degraded in these latter days; there are signs that the world is speedily coming to an end. Bribery and corruption are common and children no longer obey their parents."

Jeremiah was not exactly a blithe spirit the morning he said:

> I looked out on earth . . . lo, all is chaos;
> I look at heaven . . . its light is gone;
> I look on the mountains . . . they are trembling;
> And all the hills are swaying!

Socrates is supposed to have complained: "The children now love luxury; they have bad manners and contempt for authority; they show disrespect for elders and love chatter in place of exercise. Children are tyrants, not the servants of their household. They no longer rise when elders enter the room. They contradict their parents, chatter before company, gobble up dainties at the table, cross their legs and tyrannize their teachers."

Had radio and television existed in Carthage in the third century, Saint Cyprian would have had more than his share of interviews. His view on the environment, politics, the military, labor and the legal system held just the right amount of imbalanced panic to suit journalists.

"The world itself now bears witness to its approaching end by the evidence of its failing powers," wrote Cyprian. "There is not so much rain in winter for fertilizing the seeds, nor in summer is there so much warmth for ripening them. The springtime is no longer so mild, nor the autumn so rich in fruit. Less marble is quarried from the exhausted mountains, and the dwindling supplies of gold and silver show that the mines are worked out and the impoverished veins of metal diminish from day to day.

"The peasant is failing and disappearing from the fields, the sailor at sea and the soldier in the camp. Uprightness in the forum, justice in the court, concord and friendship, skill in the arts and discipline in morals are all disappearing. Can anything that is old preserve the same powers that it had in the prime and vigor of its youth?"

In the early nineteenth century, Goethe said all of that in a sentence: "I thank God I am not young in such a thoroughly finished world."

Sensibilities change but there clings to the human spirit, like a morning fog, the need for nostalgia. And some disappointment with the present. And fear for the future. The Greeks were right—to keep a balance in all of this is one of the hardest things in life.

Saint Augustine showed a remarkable balance in his caring and not caring when he received word in Carthage that Rome had been sacked by the barbarians. The news pained him greatly, but he said: "Let us remember that if it has happened, then God has permitted it."

The great Spanish mystic, Teresa of Avila, showed a similar attitude: "Let us not cast blame upon the times, for it is always a good age for God to give great favors to those who truly serve him."

Malcolm Muggeridge said that the sentence that most influenced his life in his latter years was from Augustine: "I no longer wished for a better world, because I was thinking of the whole of creation, and in the light of this clearer discernment I had come to see that, though the higher things are better than the lower, the sum of all creation is better than the higher things alone."

Although Carl Sagan, the astronomer, says he is not

a believer, he seems to agree with Augustine. "As for my-self," wrote Sagan, "I like a universe that includes much that is unknown and, at the same time, much that is knowable. A universe in which everything is known would be static and dull, as boring as the heaven of some weak-minded theologians. A universe that is unknowable is no fit place for a thinking being. The ideal universe for us is one very much like the universe we inhabit. And I would guess that this is not really much of a coincidence!"

The clearer discernment of mysticism is an over-brimming grace. Awe comes with it, and, as someone said, wonder is the basis of worship. Those of us who are not mystics might draw some awe and wonder from sci-ence and gain a sense of symmetry that will direct our caring and not caring.

In searching the cosmos—the very word means or-der, design—astronomers estimate that there are some 400 billion suns in our galaxy alone. And the universe contains as many as 100 billion galaxies. So every person who ever lived could have several galaxies to play with.

And distance! From the core of our galaxy to its outer reaches is about 30,000 light years. (A single light year is a distance of roughly six trillion miles.)

It is through such creation and not from a burning bush that God speaks. As the psalmist knew: "The heav-ens declare the glory of God." The galaxies reveal a uni-versal order that speaks of the awesome symmetry of God.

Carl Sagan, in his book *Broca's Brain*, speaks of such symmetry and illustrates it with an anecdote about the Scottish physicist James Clerk Maxwell who set down four mathematical equations based on the work of Michael Faraday and felt uneasy about them. "The equations exhibited a curious lack of symmetry, and this bothered Maxwell," wrote Sagan. "There was something unaesthetic about the equations as then known. . . ."

To improve the symmetry, Maxwell added something based on his intuition. The addition had astonishing consequences. The corrected equations, said Sagan, implied the existence of electromagnetic radiation, encompassing gamma rays, x-rays, ultraviolet light, visible light, infrared and radio. This led to a technical revolution: electric lights, telephone, phonograph, radio, television, cardiac pacemaker, subway, electronic computer, to name a few. Maxwell's corrected equations also stimulated Einstein to discover Special Relativity. All because a man's aesthetic sense was disturbed by an imbalance. And it may be out of an aesthetic sense that Eliot prayed for the symmetry of "teach us to care and not to care."

Science is revelation in our time. When the trillions of cells in our bodies get steeped in the things which science reveals, we ought to at least stand at the edge of mysticism. Once steeped in awe and wonder we may, like Augustine, be resigned to the difference between tactics, those fragments of life we can do something about, and strategy, that great flow of reality beyond our tampering.

The mystic with clearer discernment, and a way of looking at time in light of eternity, ought to bring a balance of sorts. And yet a mystic's way of caring and not caring is apt to be misunderstood in our time, perhaps in any time. Activists will almost surely scorn it as indifference.

It even takes balance to admit that in your own life

you cannot completely solve the problem of unity, variety, harmony and balance. It will take all of your imagination, creativity, common sense and personal discipline to shape each day into a part of your magnum opus.

No matter how well you design life it just won't be heaven on earth. What Job said still holds: "Man born of woman is of brief days and full of care." And yet if you live so that whatever you do seems fitting for the season, death should come as a fulfillment, the last step in a long procession of "rightness." Within the happy life there is a movement toward wholeness.

Early in life is the time to start getting ready for a well-designed old age. The young need to develop inner resources that carry through the years, along with imagination, sensitivity, curiosity and other characteristics of a lively spirit. Ecclesiastes says: "The things that thou hast not gathered in youth, how shall thou find them in old age?"

Santayana, in his eighties, feared that blindness might cause him to be bored for the first time in his life. He hoped to lighten the dark days by translating into various languages the Greek and Latin poems he had committed to memory in youth. It was a kind of insurance policy, one not offered at Hartford.

Insurance policies can't prepare the inner self for old age because no one can hand you the truly good life all packaged. You must design it for yourself: Are you a socializer or a loner? Is your health robust or diminished? Are you rich, poor, or somewhere in between? What fits your nature and circumstance? What feels "right" for you? And what best helps you remember God?

6

May Your Soul Catch Up

On an African safari the native bearers, after moving at a swift pace all morning, suddenly refused to go another step. "No, they are not tired," said the head-bearer, "nor are they afraid of what looms ahead."

"Then why are you stopping?" asked the explorer.

"We have traveled fast," said the head-bearer, "and we must now wait for our souls to catch up."

The leisure enjoyed in old age may allow your soul to catch up. Then, more than at any other time of life, it is possible to be yourself. In school you may have played the game to "pass" and later played it to make a living. Retirement frees you from all of that.

As any old man can tell you, a long life in itself is no blessing. It all depends on how you use the added years. The quality of each day is more important than the quantity of years. Lives lack quality when they never jell, never take shape. The admirable life, even during leisure time, is purposeful, not arbitrary.

By leisure I don't mean fun-and-games, or amusement, or idleness, but something freely chosen that puts purpose into your life. Leisure is an extension of your vocation. Marcus Aurelius was describing a vocation when he spoke of "doing the things for which I exist and for which I was brought into the world."

Some old people fail to find a good use for leisure because they see themselves as products of their past rather than as creators of their present. They have not even said goodbye to the dependency of childhood. It is easier to point to others with blame than to straighten up and do something worth doing. They failed to learn that one grows only through *élan vital*, the vital upthrust of ongoing life.

Old people need to "look to today." They might look back with pleasure from time to time, and look ahead, too, but just a little way. They need still to keep their noses pressed firmly against the Now.

One is barely conscious of the Now, if living only in memory or in anticipation. It is a good exercise to make the moment work. Be aware of sounds, and smells and tastes. Give attention to the instant.

To fret over the past is foolish. As a character says in George Eliot's *Adam Bede:* "It's but little good you do a-watering the last year's crop." Besides, too many people put a better light on the past than it deserves.

To fret too much about the future is also foolish. The cemetery is filled with people who worried about catastrophe overtaking them only to have death arrive first.

Appreciate the moment, but don't cling to it, either. Don't cling to anything. That is a part of leisure.

As for the best use of leisure, you will have to discover that yourself. As Adrian Van Kaam wrote: "We must rid our minds of the idea that any expert knows ultimately better than we ourselves how to live our lives. Surely, he may tell you how the average man lives his life and what endangers happiness. We should heed such information. What the expert cannot tell us is how to make this information operational in the unique situation of our personal lives. There we alone are the experts. We alone are responsible."

Another psychologist observed that in trying to make life easier for the elderly, "well meaning do-gooders often hasten their decline." When do-gooders, full of sentimentality, write about the elderly they almost always begin by complaining that we live in a youth-oriented society where old age is not given its due regard. Articles written and laws passed and federal guidelines issued will not gain respect for old people by one iota. Only old people can do that for themselves. If they live admirable lives—using leisure in an admirable way—they will be respected. Respect comes from doing something that others hold in high regard.

Activities of the aged may well evolve from a lifelong vocation. A ninety year old optometrist visits schools to test the eyes of children. A former newspaperman shows charitable organizations how to get their messages heard. An aging athlete coaches in a neighborhood park. They know they are moving in the right direction if they find satisfaction in their leisure.

Those who don't know how to use the hours of leisure focus on themselves. This brings on self-pity and leads to bitterness and complaining, like the terrible wailing that assails the ears at sunrise in the jungles of Borneo as monkeys complain about another day that they will have to survive. Ninety-eight percent of our genes are like those of chimpanzees, but the special two percent that lifts us above them does not deter human complainers. As Dr. Johnson said of Dryden, he knows how to complain. Many old people are "Drydenites." They rake-and-bag ailments with satisfaction. They cherish each neurosis, sensing that if self-pity is taken from them, they will have difficulty filling all of that empty space.

What they need is to get up in the morning feeling in possession of the day. If nothing helps put the hours in motion, they will feel captives of time, dragging from sunrise to sunset. If they avoid making a decision by doing nothing, that, too, is a decision and may be the hardest of all.

In old age complainers give over their lives to their feelings. What they feel is important, of course, but *doing* is what brings satisfaction. So they feel and feel and feel, never getting up and moving toward something. They could be doing any of a thousand things: planting a garden, learning a language, painting a picture. When they avoid activity, at the end of the day they suffer the deadly tiredness of those who do nothing.

Just for a start they might do something about the room in which they spend most of their time. That room is not just a physical fact; it is also the reflection of a state of mind. And it will influence attitudes.

When Florence Nightingale wrote some notes on nursing in 1860, she was aware of the effect of environment: "The effect in sickness of beautiful objects and variety of objects, and especially of color, is hardly at all appreciated."

She explained that beautiful objects influence both mind and body and urged nurses to be aware of this. "Variety of form and brilliance of color in the objects presented to patients are actually means of recovery."

When I interviewed Sister Madeleva, C.S.C., the president of Saint Mary's College, for a magazine article, she said: "Do you want to know something about me? Look at this room. It has been my study for twenty-five years. It will tell you much about me."

And so it did. It reflected charm, cultivation, imagination and elegance, all characteristics that Sister Madeleva enjoyed in abundance. Just to walk into that room lifted the spirit.

Things labeled as "problems of aging" are really problems of living no matter what the age. Those pessimistic at seventy were that way at forty; age only intensified the flaw. Such negative people, cherishing the bottomless well of grievances, find that the years dim everything except their resentments. Eventually they become controlling-old-people and there is nothing more ugly. Had they created a life of their own they would not be trying to control others.

Failing to find a good way to spend leisure is a serious matter because if you fail you squander time and remain estranged from your most valuable self, the real self, the person you are capable of being down where the soul abides. You need to be different from everyone gone before or coming after, a unique individual and not part of a cookie-cutter mediocrity.

Anyone failing to grow as an individual becomes what Ortega y Gasset called a "mass man." The mass man thinks that bigger is best and goes with the crowd. Being fascinated by fads he provides the mass audience for best

sellers, big box office, the top ten, and, in general, promotes mass movements. He is found on crowded highways, in screaming arenas, and in seething shopping
centers. His excessive wants spoil the environment. To
cater to his excesses, trees fall, asphalt covers grass, and
noise fills all available space. Although highly active the
mass man is never really original and misses being one-
of-a-kind.

Individuality has something to do with happiness,
the kind nobody can give you for your birthday. Happiness is more than a flight from unhappiness. You realize
that whenever you are in the wonderfully alive presence
of a happy person. The collective pursuit of happiness is
a delusion; the happy soul is an individual who is apt to
know the good uses of leisure.

When old people have a hard time finding a good use
for leisure, the chances are that they have led "borrowed"
lives. A young woman, for instance, said that she is going
to study to be a welder because "I hear there is good
money in it." Another young woman leading a borrowed
life said that she is keeping at a job she hates because she
has "three days off a week." Another woman upon grad-
uating from college with high honors said that she had
long aspired to be a doctor but "medicine would be a poor
return on my investment," and so she decided on a career
as an investment banker.

Those three young women will do work that is worth
doing but for the wrong reason. They are looking for "a
good deal." All work, even the meanest, has value for the
inner self but only if done as a vocation instead of as a job.

Since the three young women are doing something

for the wrong reasons, they may eventually feel that they belong more to the work than to themselves. The work never becomes a part of them. In surrounding themselves with barriers of their own making they risk narrowness. Financially, they may end up looking good, but they will pay a hidden price.

Upon retirement those who led borrowed lives sometimes turn to a mad pursuit of leisure that is little more than a distraction from the certainty of death. It is sad when the elderly spend their time fiddling around with activities that just wallpaper empty spaces inside themselves. In time they move toward a malaise that saps their vitality even though a battery of lab tests declares them healthy. Health is more than the absence of disease; it includes leading a life worth leading. What's more, those who suffer a sense of dis-ease with life may find dis-ease waiting in the wings. Spiritual downness lowers the barriers throughout the body, giving unhealthy things a chance to take over.

With the misuse of leisure boredom sets in and destroys, like termites, not in a dramatic way but with hidden, persistent, silent crumbling. Like the Santa Ana wind the days grate on bored people leaving them feeling close to the edge. Such ennui is best avoided by being absorbed in something that not only encourages bodily movement, but starts a new current of life in the soul.

Since boredom is a deadly infection stay clear of it. When coming upon those suffering from it—upset, toxic, annoying—hurry in the opposite direction. If infected you, too, will become unhappy and attract unhappy people, those who have a way of making life banal, of turning wine into water. Soon you and the unhappy ones will be looking for things to make you happy, not realizing that happiness comes as a by-product and is not something to be aimed at, or even thought about.

Some gerontologists predict that science will find a way to prolong life almost indefinitely. Considering the life bored people lead, that will be a horrible sentence.

In old age, death takes friends out of your life fast enough; so don't drive them away with boredom. Most people need friends to share in their leisure. Books have been written about how to make friends, but to say to yourself, "Today I will choose a new friend," seems artificial. Making friends usually begins with meeting someone who vibrates on your wavelength, and, presto, you are on the verge of a new closeness.

Everybody needs enough friends to help build a fire against the darkness. Some need many friends because they find that being alone for even a short time brings on loneliness. That is especially true of those who have gone through life depending on others, or expecting others to depend on them.

For some people aloneness is wonderful. To be able to enjoy your own company, without being preoccupied with self, is a gift. Withdrawal, though—that is another matter; there could be warpedness in that.

Friends and conversations go together. Real conversation, a part of leisure, is satisfying and refreshing. In it you find yourself taking pleasure in the mind of another. There is a difference between chatter and conversation, between yackety-yak and talking about something at some altitude. Good conversation is not trivial: the subject matter is worth talking about, observations are not banal, gossip is absent, and the method of expression reflects imagination and some style.

When you can no longer take an active part in the life of the tribe you tend to become talkative. Someone said of an old man that he sat around recapitulating the dull incidents of his life until he finally got as tired as his listeners and went ahead and died. A defense against such garrulousness is to learn to listen. Alexander Korda said that as a boy in Budapest he learned to be a good talker, but years later in Berlin he learned to listen. "You have to be older for that," he said. Both good conversation and good listening are a part of leisure. The play of mind against mind can make for a wonderful friendship.

When you have reached the age when you are like the marked tree in a woods, you can still do more than merely wait. It is a good idea to try to do something each day that will stick in the memory. Otherwise, days become blurred reproductions of each other. Gray year follows gray year and contributes nothing to a memorable life. Of course you need to do something trivial from time to time, but to make an avocation of the trivial is demeaning. A priest said, "Don't let them trivialize your retirement. Entertainment is the lowest form of using leisure."

The Indian poet, Tagore, gave leisure an exalted place when he wrote: "Civilizations are wealths that have been harvested from the deep and of leisure." Adding your part to civilizing influences is an admirable way to spend your latter days.

To keep leisure time from becoming empty some

sort of second career is the answer. Leisure in retirement brings your last chance to follow your natural bent, to do the thing you have been hankering to do—study psychology, start a boutique, review books, or any of a thousand other possibilities.

Creative activity has great therapeutic value. If you urge such activity on people they beg-off by saying they lack the talent for writing, painting, composing. But there are many ways of being creative: baking biscuits from scratch, building a bookcase, cultivating roses. When someone asked Voltaire if he had lived a life worth living he said, "Yes, I planted 4,000 trees."

No matter what you do, however, you will feel let down from time to time. "The most exalted," said Lacardaire, "succumb to the mysterious poison of disappointment." An American Olympic skater, Scott Hamilton, learned this truth of life quite young. He said that on the day he won the gold medal he felt sad. No matter what you do, you will say from time to time, "Is this all there is?"

Old people, prone to being weighted down with melancholy and foreboding, are more apt to suffer a spiritual than an economic crisis. The best defense is to show concern for the spirit as part of a growth in leisure. Deep within the spirit, covered by the debris of a cluttered life, are seeds that could bloom. In London during the blitz, seeds that had been buried for three hundred years propagated themselves, when bombed to the surface, and made displays of purple milkworth and willow herb. The vicar of Saint James Piccadilly counted twenty-three varieties behind his bombed altar. If the trauma of senescence brings good things to light, the last of life becomes a time to refind and refine the soul.

Neither will this come as a constant consolation. Spiritual experience happens in short flights—flickers and flashes in darkness, a musical phrase in silence. To get through arid days you need the acceptance expressed by a Chinese philosopher: "Human life is such that the moon cannot always be round, the flowers cannot always look so fine, and good friends cannot always meet together." He might have added that the silence of God is not always easy to endure.

Leisure at its best is concerned with the marvelous. Such concerns bring a sense of wonder, and wonder is the basis of worship. The whole of life seems sacramental when you see all of creation charged with wonder and mystery. A French writer, Jean Guitton, said of Lord Halifax: "Life for him was the most stimulating, mysterious, delicate, romantic, variegated and zestful thing imaginable. His constant exclamations were, 'Isn't it exciting; isn't it strange!'"

Responding with such zest to the surprises of life is a grace. Creation gives a magnificent performance; if you really "see" you will never be bored. Knowledge reveals such beauty that to study sciences—biology, physics, chemistry—could be an aesthetic experience, a thrill of the spirit that comes when in the presence of the awesome.

A mathematician might look at a sheet of paper with a few marks on it and thrill to the revelation of an elegant and marvelous concept. A non-mathematician, not ready for the concept, looks at the same sheet of paper and feels bored. Much of life is unnecessarily boring; the thing to do is to use leisure to get ready for more of life's amazements.

Such readiness develops a sense of awe. The greatest compliment you can pay an artist is to admire his work, so perhaps the greatest form of worship is to stand in awe of creation. A book of astronomy with its definiteness might bring more of a lift to your spirit than a book of theology.

With old age comes more time for reflection, meditation, contemplation. For such "consideration," as Saint Bernard of Clairvaux called it, you need time free from distraction. At a remote place in Korea an old priest told me that the leisure of retirement, at its best, brings readiness for "the coming of God." It is fitting, he felt, that the elderly, more than the young, be aware of the "scent" of God that permeates the universe.

7

Latter-Day Students

Years ago, before planning on growing old, I waited in a barber shop while an elderly gentleman got a haircut. From his conversation with the barber I learned that he was a retired executive from a local industry.

"Bet you can't guess what I'm doing?" he said to the barber. "I'm going to school."

"What you studying?"

"French and Spanish."

"How you doing?"

"Better than expected. Better than the young students. I have more time to study."

A decade later, at age forty-two, I also went back to school. While teaching full-time I took graduate courses for five years and was surprised to find myself a better student by far than I had been twenty years earlier. I was better able to separate the important from the unimportant and get to the heart of things. With more "realization" I came to agree with Leonardo that "the noblest pleasure is the joy of understanding."

So I am not surprised to hear that Columbia University, Iowa State College, and the University of Michigan have found that the ability to learn improves with time.

To test the learning ability of older people, Columbia enrolled 270 men and women between ages forty-five and seventy to study the Russian language. Most felt that they were too old to tackle a new language, but agreed to give it their best. They met for two hours a day; at the end of eight weeks they were as far along as the undergraduates at the end of a fourteen-week semester.

Dr. Irving Lorge, who conducted the experiment, concluded: "The years do far less damage to our mental capacity than has been supposed. What happened to our minds has less to do with the birthdays than with how well we used our minds through life."

At Iowa State College a professor tracked down 127 alumni who had taken the Army's Alpha Mental Ability Test more than thirty years earlier. He gave them the same test and found that they scored better than they had at eighteen.

The professor, William A. Owens, observed: "Nowhere was there a sign that brains had grown rusty. On the contrary, the increase in most mental capacities was tremendous. Most impressive of all was an increase in scores in certain categories where logic and clear thinking are required. The inescapable conclusion is that most people are smarter at fifty."

A gerontologist at the University of Michigan, Dr. Wilma Donohue, announced that there is good evidence that the greater the intellectual endowment and the greater the amount of education, the less steep the decline in the intellect. She said that the ability of the brain to continue active and grow in stature is a remarkable phenomenon. Although there is a certain amount of structural deterioration, there is not a concomitant loss of function.

A statement from the National Association for Mental Health said: "Mental slowdown doesn't go along with aging in the same way as physical slowdown. Unless a real disease prevents circulation in the brain, mental slowdown is so slight, so extremely gradual that it's hardly worth thinking about."

If all of this sounds out of touch with reality, let me admit that advanced age does take some toll of the mind. In speaking of a ninety-four year old woman someone described her as "sharp," meaning she is remarkable for her age, but I doubt that she is as keen as she was a couple of decades earlier.

Several regrettable things can happen in advanced age. The mind might flit like a butterfly with nothing holding its interest for long: a return to childhood when attention was ever on the wing. Or the mind grows opaque gradually, the way vision blurs beneath a cataract. Or it goes suddenly, bang, like an old tire that has lost elasticity.

Since decline is inevitable the problem is not to avoid it, but to slow it down. The decline slows when the mind is kept active, and so the moral is: Keep learning. That is the way for you to be enriched by time instead of degraded by it.

Dr. Milton Gumpert, a specialist in geriatrics, said that throughout history there have been heroic examples of old people maintaining productivity while most of their contemporaries slipped into senility. The productive ones, he said, "handled their lives as a continuous unit of mental and emotional development, by never retiring, by never ceasing to learn."

The pleasures of the mind ought to be cultivated throughout life. It is not realistic to expect someone to begin having intellectual interests in old age if there was none there before. As Dr. Wilma Donohue observed, you have a better chance for an interesting old age if you are educated. This brings up the question of what is education.

We tend to think of education as learning something; real education is *becoming* something. Education may begin in school but the development of self, the becoming, is a lifelong work. We used to speak of "girls' finishing schools," and good things they were, but everybody needs finishing, a lifetime of it, to acquire some polish.

Our lives are always "not yet." We are on the move, always "becoming" for good or for ill. We tend to think of ourselves as complete, static, congealed, set once and for all. But we are on a journey whether we will or no. There is no stopping at the guest house.

Some people absorb much schooling along the way but precious little education. A college degree requires schooling—many hours in the classroom—but there is no guarantee that every diploma-bearer is educated. It is possible to memorize answers and play them back letter-perfect during exams without developing an abiding interest in things of mind and spirit. The uneducated lack a desire to keep learning.

The possibility of education comes after the passing of a certain number of years. Mortimer Adler said: "The young cannot be educated. Youth is the obstacle." He observed that youth is trainable, but only mature adults can be educated. Most of the things that bring maturity occur after leaving school.

"The business of getting married," Adler said, "of having children, of having our parents become ill, or dependent on us, or die, the death of friends, our business and social responsibilities—these are the things that age us. And aging is part of what makes us mature."

This need for the passing of time shows up in all walks of life. For example, Sir Laurence Olivier said in an interview with Kenneth Tynan, in the New York Times: "But Macbeth is another problem altogether. I mean if you are, say, twenty-seven years old, you can't do it. You can recite it, you can go through the motions, you give them a hell of a fight at the end, you can reach all sorts of poetic passages, but only to a certain degree, because you have to be of a certain maturity to play parts as enormous as that."

The thing is to grow with maturity, to better appreciate beauty, to stand in awe of mystery, and to feel a reverence for the things God made. A scarcity of those inner resources reflects a lack of education. With such poverty of mind and spirit, old people may complain of financial poverty without good reason. They know something is lacking and have to put the blame somewhere.

In his *Moral Epistles*, Seneca said: "I only recommend retirement to you if you use it for greater and more beautiful activities." He knew that old age is no time to become trivial, that you still need some sense of purpose, something to feel proud of at the end of the day. He may have observed that nothing more readily separates interesting people from bores than their response to retirement.

My generation knows better than my father's how to find a satisfying retirement. His generation thought of old age solely as a time of subtractions, but we are learning that there can be some additions as well. The next generation will be still better prepared for retirement because schools are paying attention to ways of developing a satisfying old age.

Some people prefer to learn on their own. Cato at eighty began studying Greek, but did not enroll in a course. Chief Justice Oliver Wendell Holmes, nearing ninety, sat himself down to a serious study of Plato, and when asked why he did so answered, "To improve my mind." In 1984 two women, one seventy-two and one eighty-eight, brought out first novels to critical acclaim; to write them they used their minds while very much alone.

Most people prefer studying in a group. In my university days a student past middle age would have caused comment if found sitting in a university classroom. Now elderly students are taken in stride. Virginia Smith, president of Vassar, said, "The students enjoy having the older students in class. And the teachers do, too."

I enjoyed having an elderly alumnus enroll in my class in design. One day I asked him if he remembered what had happened thirty-eight years ago that very day: the day he had given me my first newspaper job. George Scheuer had finished at Notre Dame in 1928 and after a career in journalism returned to the campus to receive an advanced degree at age seventy.

In this part of the country older people are being encouraged to return to the classroom and surely that must be happening all over. This important step in their lives is made easy for them at Notre Dame, Saint Mary's College, Holy Cross Junior College, Indiana University at South Bend, and Bethel College.

Father Louis Putz, C.S.C., a retired member of the Notre Dame faculty, began a school for people fifty-five or older. He started the Forever Learning Institute in 1974 in the Bendix mansion. Forty courses are offered to the students. Many of the teachers are retired Notre Dame professors.

Notre Dame joined the Elderhostel Movement four years ago, a movement that has spread across the United States in the past dozen years. The combining of adult education with hosteling started at the University of New Hampshire in 1974. The movement attracts each year about 60,000 students sixty or over, who spend three weeks living in college dorms and taking courses from the college faculty.

The scope of study is as wide as the world and as vast as the universe. Philosophy, literature, science and art are among the possibilities.

Philosophy is a study especially apt for late in life. Plato said that no one should try to deal with it until age thirty. Maybe he exaggerated for the sake of effect, but he realized it is best not to roam among abstractions until bumping one's head against enough concrete things. It is difficult to speak of "a twenty year old philosopher" without smiling.

As for the value of literature it, too, is a study that

grows in value the more hours you breathe on earth. F. Scott Fitzgerald said in *Beloved Infidel:* "That is part of the beauty of all literature. You discover that your longings are universal longings, that you're not lonely and isolated from anyone. You belong."

When you study science late in life you may finally see it as revelation in our time. You can't help but stand in awe of creation upon learning that your heart supplies blood to the body through 60,000 miles of plumbing, and that our galaxy is made up of about a hundred billion stars and that billions of such planetary systems exist, and that the Rand Corporation estimates that there are about 640,000 earth-type planets in our galaxy—planets enough like ours to sustain life as we know it.

Learning such things brings awe and wonder for what God has done. You realize how small you are and yet feel bigger than ever because you are proud to have a role to play in the Great Script.

Since you should not just grow older but should also *grow*, a study of the arts can be helpful. Socrates exclaimed, "Surely the aim and consummation of all education is the love of loveliness." This is not always stressed in schools where ways of making a living are pursued. When, however, you have put earning a living behind you, there is no reason not to learn the love of loveliness.

Travel can also be highly instructive. It attracts many retirees but quite a few get little from it; they are going through life with blinkers on their eyes and stoppers in their ears, not really seeing anything or hearing anything. Their opinions are a set of rubber-stamp clichés kept filed away inside a narrow mind. Whenever something new turns up, be it a painting or a play, a political program or an insight into theology, they reach inside for one of the clichés and rubber-stamp the object and withdraw to the cell of their complacency.

If you want to witness this attitude at its most dramatic, watch the tourists. They get up enough nerve to leave home in body, but many lack the courage to leave in spirit. Jets help them change the landscape all around them but the landscape of their minds never alters. They are annoyed with the unfamiliar, be it a brand of coffee, the plumbing, or cultural patterns. They want the whole universe paved just like the street they live on.

They walk through castles and museums and cathedrals and are bored. If they were as aware of their sagging spirits as they are of their aching feet, it would be a hopeful sign. The sense of awe is dried up in them and they seldom show wonder, unless you want to count the many times a day they say, "I wonder how far away the bus is parked?"

One good thing about travel is that it retards the flight of time. Ionesco said: "Two days of traveling and the sight of a new city does slow down the racing flow of events. Two days in a new country are worth thirty lived in familiar surroundings, thirty days worn and shortened, spoiled and damaged by habit. Habit polishes them—you slip as you do on an over-waxed floor."

Most days, in old age, bring no new things into our lives. Most of what happens we have seen before. A fresh experience is worth searching for because a day that brings something new is usually remembered. To collect

memorable days, that's the thing! An historian wrote of
the Duke of Urbino: "The Duke was ever careful to learn
some new thing every day."

If you cannot afford a trip, or if like certain old wines
you do not travel well, the journey for fresh experience
may be wholly inward. Books can bring new experiences
daily and they are free at the public library.

A Norwegian at ninety-nine was still active on skies
and in a canoe. In a documentary film he said: "I've always wanted to know what is on the other side of the hill."
That is a good theme for anyone's life. Whether the journey to the other side of the hill is made in formal classes,
or in personal study, or in a library, or on trips abroad,
the important thing is the fresh experience. Pindar put it
in a sentence: "With God's help may I still love what is
beautiful and strive for what is attainable."

8

The High Calling of a Pedestrian

One of the best uses of leisure in retirement is walking. I learned quite young that walking puts me in touch with the moods of all times of day and all turns of season. As a student I knew what Soren Kierkegaard meant in admonishing: "Above all, do not lose your desire to walk. Every day I walk myself into a state of well-being, and walk away from every illness. I have walked myself into my best thoughts, and I know of no thought so burdensome that one cannot walk away from it."

While gathering material for *Why Americans Retire Abroad* I met an elderly New Yorker who explained why he had retired to the Costa del Sol in Southern Spain: "Here I can walk every day. In New York that was not possible. When you get my age you must walk *every* day!"

As he and I plodded in deep sand along the Mediterranean, the feisty little fellow said that the older you get the quicker inactivity leads to atrophy. With grim zest he described how muscles waste, bones lose calcium, and the flow of digestive juices turns sluggish.

All the way to Torremolinos he delivered a lecture on how walking promotes the blood's circulation, soothes nerves and lubricates the joints. He was so knowledgeable about the workings of the body that I asked him if he was a medical doctor. No, he said, he had made his fortune in the New York garment district, but knows the values of walking, because he has read nearly everything written on the subject.

He was full of quotes:

"Action absorbs anxiety."

"Your body is the one machine that breaks down when *not* used."

"The chief cause of overweight is not gluttony but sloth."

It was evident that the energetic little man saw me as a possible convert. I let it go at that. No use ruining his lecture by telling him that each year I log more miles on foot than in an automobile.

Long before our walk on the Costa del Sol I had come to know that one of the healthiest things you can do on this remote planet is to aspire to the high calling of a pedestrian. Yet that is not why I, as the Book of Job puts it, walk up and down in the land and to and fro on the earth.

When walking I am often asked, "Are you taking your constitutional?" or "Getting your exercise?" My nod of assent does not really tell the truth. To do anything for exercise alone, such as take calisthenics, seems boring.

I walk for results not measured by instruments. What a walk does for the spirit is more important than what it does for the cardiovascular system.

On days when there is no opportunity to walk, I miss the state of mind more than the exercise. On walkless days I taught less well and now I write less well. As Sydney Smith observed long ago: "You shall never break down in a speech on the day on which you have walked twelve miles."

Something about walking stimulates thought, soothes the soul and smoothes out a rumpled psyche. While putting one foot in front of another the cosmos does not seem so near collapse as when sitting before a TV set watching the evening news. The end is not yet.

I am a saunterer. My style is best described by the German verb *bummeln* and the French verb *flaner* meaning to amble along, to wander around in a city at leisure, without definite aim, enjoying the sights, human and architectural. This passing show is so enchanting that I rarely go to watch something conjured up inside a theater.

Edwin Way Teale said that for a naturalist the slower the walk the better. He must see, and not *just* see, but appreciate and feel.

I heard of a man who used to enjoy the adventure of a "zig-zag walk." He would take the first turn left, the next right, and the next left, and on and on. In strange cities I used to do a modified version: at intersections I looked ahead and to the right and to the left and selected the direction that held most promise. Within an hour I was thoroughly lost, of course, but a map always saved me.

To step out, with map in hand, into a sunny morning in an interesting city does much for the inner man. Momentarily, the world is transfigured, life is aglow, and human beings seem worth saving.

Some places make me more alert, more receptive to life than others. I can measure this almost scientifically by counting the number of 3 × 5 cards filled each day. The more alert I feel the more notes get scribbled on the cards carried in my jacket pocket, and it is from such cards that books and articles get written.

My most cherished memories of trips have something to do with walks. There are a few good memories of trains (the Twentieth Century Limited and the Blue Train) and of ships (the Queen Elizabeth and the Queen Mary) but I cannot dredge up one happy memory of airplanes, buses or automobiles.

I rate cities by how they are for walking. Among favorites are Salzburg, Venice and Kyoto; the least favorites are Tokyo, Los Angeles, and Calcutta. Until New York turned shabby it was a wonderful city for walking. The great cities of Paris, London, and Rome have been so spoiled by maniac drivers that crossing an intersection in any of them is like playing Russian roulette.

These days when roads are no longer roads but arteries, hardened arteries, a walk in the country can be as dangerous as a walk in town. Roadways are not a part of our democracy because drivers, in their disdain for pedestrians, have declared this world their own beyond dispute. Too bad, because a walker is unobtrusive; he does not spoil the mood of a place with noise and fumes the way a motorist does.

Even the back roads in Ireland are dangerous now. Up to twenty years ago they were a delight, but cars have taken over there as they did here years ago. So you proceed with caution down crooked lanes, between stone fences, facing oncoming traffic, ready to jump into the roadside tangle. When such self-preservation becomes the dominant emotion you are not enjoying the kind of walk that might help you repossess your soul. It is not one that leads inward to the land of your better self.

How sad, for when on foot there can be an intimacy with trees, streams, cows and any minor poets that you meet along the way. Had William Blake been facing traffic, or commuting bumper-to-bumper, he would not have had the vision which could see a world in a grain of sand, and a heaven in a wild flower.

A walk outside of town reveals the real horror of the approaches to our cities. They all look alike: surrealistic stretches of blatant signs, cement block buildings, used car lots. While in such a chaotic setting never try to cross four lanes on foot. In an Italian film a woman does just that while her husband cringes at the side of the freeway. As she reaches safety, she pants, "It takes great courage to cross the road."

Walking on a paved surface has some advantages, but walking on God's good earth is more interesting; the feel of it is not so monotonous as an artificial surface. The trouble is that walking on the shoulders of a road has become an invitation to lockjaw and blood poisoning; they are fetlock deep in broken bottles and rusting beer cans.

Notre Dame is still a wonderful place for walking. The campus, especially around the lakes, changes its mood with time of day and season of the year. My favorite is autumn when trees seem to give out a light of their own, yellow, orange, and scarlet.

There are interesting creatures to visit too: the white owl near the grotto, red wing blackbirds behind Columba Hall, and the loon in the lake near the log chapel. When walking up Notre Dame Avenue one dawn I saw an elegant silhouette behind the golf course fence midway between the cemetery and the inn. My suspicion was that students had lifted an ornamental deer from the lawn of a mansion and put it there on the fairway. No sooner did I have such an uncharitable thought than a graceful doe took three great leaps and disappeared into the mists.

Early morning with its freshness has always been my favorite time. An evening walk had some virtues but those are canceled out now by threats of crime. Yet neither threat of crime nor bad weather can stay some of us from our appointed rounds. We have inside us the need to walk, a primitive urge perhaps that has something to do with ancestors calling across the centuries.

Many people find walking uncongenial; they act as though it is immoral. Their motto seems to be: Always park the car as near to the door as possible. College administrators answered many questions in a national survey; the section on parking problems makes discouraging reading: "No one wants to walk more than fifty feet. They are reluctant to walk any distance to their home building. They all want to park alongside their desks."

I have seen students trying to hitch a ride to class when well within the confines of the campus. Perhaps that is because they grew up in a motorized culture, one that smeared blacktop across the fields of my childhood and destroyed places where wild flowers used to grow.

A traumatic experience, a sudden confinement, can help one see walking in a new light. For instance, during his final stay in the hospital, Professor Richard Sullivan spoke with gratitude about his doctor, Louis Sandock.

His face lit up when he said: "Louis did a nice thing the other day. He told a nurse to take me outside and wheel me down to the corner. My, but it was nice!" He was realizing how lovely a trip to the corner can be.

Elisabeth Kübler-Ross said that her values have been influenced by her work with the dying: "I know that to see a winter sunset or to watch a pheasant family stroll the lawn is infinitely more important than material things."

One day when I came near death in an accident there was a brightness, a brillance, an illumination about the hour that I never knew before and have not experienced since. Everything seemed more important than usual. From the ambulance I saw two nurses walking, laughing, in a little park, and a butcher painting the prices of sausage on his shop window. Their ability to move about seemed a remarkable thing to be able to do. All the while I was aware that had I been killed the nurses would be laughing anyway, and the butcher would still be concentrating on his window.

Such enlightenment, such resurrection, was better described in an article that Robert Payne wrote about André Malraux. After Malraux's plane had been shot down he was driven into Bone where he found the place miraculously transformed, so that everything appeared larger than life and strangely beautiful.

"He was fascinated by the processes of resurrection. Just to see some chickens pecking in the dawn light was to be aware of an illumination; the flight of pigeons swerving and turning white in the sun filled him with wonder. This small abandoned village in Flanders, with its kennels and rabbit hutches and wash hanging on the line, was exquisitely perfect in the purity of the morning air, and the war seemed far away. For him it was like entering a new country for the first time. It was a magical country, and he would not have been surprised if all the farm animals had begun to speak."

In that morning of miracles Malraux was seeing the world as seen in a Chagall painting. From that day on he was ready to agree with Rilke: "If your daily round seems unrewarding, don't put the blame on it; blame yourself for not being able to evoke the riches that are to be found in it."

The writer said that when Malraux entered the village that morning "it was like entering a new country for the first time." You see something for the first time only once. You cannot repeat the thrill of recognition felt at first sight of the Parthenon sitting so thoroughly on the hill, or the noble dome of Saint Peter's against a blue sky, or the cathedral of Notre Dame, with its bristle of buttresses, over there across the Seine. The thrill of seeing them may come again, but without that first freshness and intensity.

I used to be interested in walking in new places, seeing things for the first time, but now I like best revisiting old ones. Since old places have changed so much you might say that I am not so interested in revisiting them as in remembering a time of life or in evoking a mood long gone.

Hal Borland said that when you have walked the same road through all seasons "you know how certain is change and how gradual." The certainty of change is worth understanding, for that is the great theme of reality.

Every place is something of a Rorschach test. You see in it only what you are ready to see. What you get from anything depends on what was locked into your genes to start with and on everything that has happened to you along the way. Maybe I am returning to places that never existed, except for me.

Lately, magazines have been running articles about the value of walking. Each causes me to recall the retired New Yorker in southern Spain. Does his shadow still fall upon the sands of the Costa del Sol?

A magazine article predicts that walkers, like joggers, will soon form a fitness cult. What to do then! I have long been alert to approaching fads and upon sighting one have turned to run in the opposite direction.

Oh Lord, at this moment in eternity don't let walking become a fad. Hold off the cultists while I still have a few miles to go.

9

The Serendipity Game

Just as retirement gives more time for walking it also gives more for reading. I try to combine both blessings by walking a mile and a half each noon from my office in the Notre Dame library to the charming new library at Saint Mary's College.

At Notre Dame I usually do research for work in progress, but at Saint Mary's I play the serendipity game. That means moving slowly along the shelves of books, always hoping for a happy discovery. The attraction might be the title, or the subject, or the author—or even the binding or the publisher. The attraction should be intuitive and not spoiled by trying to play it too smart. You must let the book find you.

While searching for a happy discovery, I take at least a dozen books from the shelf to find one worthy of some remaining part of my life. Although most powers dim with age, the power of choice grows stronger; now I am better able to select a good book, a good painting, a good anything. When the right book comes to hand I go to a rocker in front of the large round window on the top floor and enjoy a Carthusian solitude.

Then back to the shelves in search for something else that has what the French call *ordonnance:* an ordered work disciplined in matter and style. As the Greeks put it, a piece of writing ought to have the feeling that nothing can be rightly added or taken away.

Jargon prevails in many books because writing with simplicity and clarity is hard business. Jo Jo Starbuck, the champion skater, said the hardest thing about developing a new routine is to make it look easy. Since many authors are not willing to pay the price of great effort to make it look easy, their books are heavy with entangled sentences that take for granted the reader has time to waste.

A French staff officer wrote such entangled sentences until Foch taught him a lesson. Whenever the staff officer presented a report, the military chief made him read it aloud. If the officer lost his breath during a marathon paragraph, or had to stop to explain its meaning, Foch ordered him to rewrite, and admonished, "Say it bluntly!" Many times, standing there in the stacks, I know how Foch felt.

Anything that wastes your time is especially annoying late in life. Henri Bergson, in old age, said that he feels like going to the street corner and start begging: "Alms, brothers! A quarter of an hour from each of you."

Now, more than in youth, I realize that a piece of writing should not just give information but should also give pleasure. What is said and how it is said are both important because the what and the how interact to produce meaning. An observation can thrill you with an insight, or put you to sleep. Information burdened with jargon beats you down; the same information presented with distinction gives a lift to the heart.

Isaac Bashevis Singer said: "In art, truth that is boring is not truth." He is right; people are boring, but truth cannot be. The very expression, a boring truth, sounds silly.

So many authors seem bored with their own writing; at least that is the feeling you get when reading it. Joubert, the French moralist, advised young authors, "Never write anything that does not give you real pleasure." If the writer is not caught up in the project, the reader will not be.

In playing the serendipity game I have developed a taste for journals, diaries, and letters, something that might not have come about through a more rational approach. With fondness I recall the journals of the Goncourt brothers, Virginia Woolf and Amiel, and Jane Austen's letters.

Fiction has become less attractive but biography and autobiography are coming more readily to hand. At the corner of my desk at this moment are *The Summing Up* by Somerset Maugham, *A Return to Yesterday* by Ford Maddox Ford, and the autobiography of Agatha Christie.

In the serendipity game, as in others, you win some and lose some. Yesterday I left the library looking forward to an evening with John Cowper Powys' autobiography and Dwight MacDonald's essays. By nightfall it was clear that I could not long abide the personalities of those two.

I first played a version of the serendipity game when I was in grade school and my sister was entering high school. Since life was not saturated with excitement on a Kentucky farm, and since the Sisters of Charity at Presentation Academy were great ones for required reading, I asked my sister to read aloud her assignments. There was chanciness in this and I kept hoping for a happy result long before hearing the word serendipity.

Perhaps the most valuable part of my education was hearing the works of Mark Twain at seven. Listening was better than reading, considering that eventually I would make a living writing. Rhythms of sentences, flavors of words, and timing of the release of ideas reach the sensibilities better through the ear than the eye.

Since there were no children on the farm my parents often sent me to visit an aunt and uncle who lived in Louisville near Shelby Park, hoping I would play there. Instead, I went right past the children and hurried to a branch of the public library to spend summer hours in cool rooms that smelled of bookbinder's paste.

Waiting there were the people of Oz, the animal friends of Doctor Doolittle and the family of Five Little Peppers. In time I came to know *Stover at Yale*, which encouraged a dream of going away to school, one that came true with a vengeance, for eventually I spent nine years as student and thirty as teacher in boarding schools.

The most happy discovery came in the summer of 1937. Shortly after being graduated from Notre Dame I worked on the night side of a South Bend newspaper and spent afternoons in the public library. There I met Mary. We were married two years later in the log chapel at Notre Dame.

During the Second World War and the Korean conflict I played the serendipity game at Fort Benning, Fort Riley, Camp Croft, Fort Bragg and small military libraries in the Far East. In peacetime I found that no matter how remote the spot on the globe the British have started a lending library there. Mary and I recall with fondness one we discovered in Palma on the island of Majorca.

No doubt about it, the serendipity game is addictive and I can't resist urging it on others. Deep in the dark reaches of any library are books nobody checks out anymore. In that literary limbo are writers who deserve to be rediscovered. For instance, George Ade and Kim Hubbard, two Hoosier humorists whose work brightened my day recently, reminding me all over again that they are funnier than owls in heaven.

Early in the century, George Ade made a reputation writing fables with such titles as "The Fable of Sister Mae, Who Did as Well as Could Be Expected." In them he wrote of the music teacher who came "to bridge that awful gap between Dorothy and Chopin," and the man "who drank like a chaperone," and of the woman who "in the mad pursuit of culture was always the first one over the fence."

In the fables you will find amusing sentences:

"She was determined to break into Society if she had to use an Ax."

"Whenever he unpacked at a Hotel he put a Photograph of Himself out on the Dresser, so as to make the Room more cheerful."

A little later in the century, Kim Hubbard was creating a character called Abe Martin, a crusty Brown County, Indiana hillbilly. Below each sketch of Abe he wrote two pointed sentences. Hubbard reasoned that if a man can make a living on two sentences a day, why write more:

"When a feller says, 'It hain't th' money, but th' principle o' th' thing,' it's th' money."

"It don't make no difference what it is, a woman'll buy anything she thinks a store is losin' money on."

"Ther' ought t'be some way t'eat celery so it wouldn't sound like you wuz steppin' on a basket."

"Jake Bently fell off a load o' hay t'day an' had t' crawl all th' way t' th' golf links t' have his leg sct."

"It's no disgrace t' be poor, but it might as well be."

"Whoever takes jest plain ginger ale soon gits drowned out o' th' conversation."

A survey, made by the University of Michigan, shows that the average American reads sixteen minutes a day—nine of the sixteen are spent on sports and comics. So when some people retire, their minds have nothing on which to feed. They were grooved, through the years, for a certain kind of work; now with retirement that groove becomes, as the British say, redundant. And since they have not been replenishing their inner selves they stare into space.

They are what Gilette Burgess called "bromides" because they put you to sleep with their predictable remarks. In an essay, Burgess wrote: "The Bromide does his thinking by syndicate. He follows the main-traveled roads, he goes with the crowd. In a word, they all think and talk alike—one may predict their opinion upon any given subject. They follow custom and costume; they obey the Law of Averages. They are, intellectually, all peas in the same conventional pod, unenlightened, prosaic, living by rule and rote."

If reading has been a minor theme in your life, it will

bring refreshing variety even into old age. No matter what your vocation, books help enlarge the narrow circle in which Nature has confined you. When walking through the stacks of a library you will feel a sense of adventure: the best minds of all time are waiting there. You feel wonderfully wealthy when you leave the building carrying books that hold promise and make you better company to have around.

One of the good things about retirement is that you have time to "give" yourself to a book. An insubstantial book you read, acting on it the way you do a lawn, but getting little in return. A substantial one acts on you, and going through it is like making a retreat.

You even have time to read and reread books of substance. While rereading you may see in yourself something more than you saw before. It is like other experiences: As you meet them coming around the carousel, you see more in them and more in yourself.

Ramon Guthrie, who taught a seminar on Marcel Proust at Dartmouth, reread *Remembrance of Things Past* each year. During the thirty-one times he went through it he never skipped any of the million-and-a-quarter words and each time he discovered something new.

In old age you more clearly hear the ring of truth. A sentence, or a conversation, or an anecdote that might have passed right by you in youth will give you pause because now you see in it a significant detail.

I now read some books that held no interest in youth. Many I began time and again but found they fired no spark, made no contact with my inner life. Trying to read them was like trying to start a car on a cold morning. Then suddenly that uninteresting book began speaking to my new self. A shadow had passed from some hidden corner of my psyche and I was ready for it. Two that I had passed over for years but responded to recently were *The Noonday Devil* by Bernard Bassett and *A Gathering of Fugitives* by Lionel Trilling.

For me one of the most satisfying pleasures is getting up at about two in the morning, reading a couple of hours, and going back to bed. There is a calmness, a solemnity, almost a reverence about that time of day.

A cup of tea, a piece of toast and one of the classics in those quiet hours when the mind is settled—what riches! Each time I do this I become aware all over again of how the classics help us sense the march of generations, the rise and fall of things, the cycle of events. They promote balance and restraint: nothing to excess. As a magnet brings unity to scattered filings, the classics draw into clusters all those filaments of facts flying around inside our heads.

This morning Horace convinced me once more that the people of two thousand years ago were every bit as alive as we are—and that the poignance of the human lot is an ever-present thing. He lived long enough to realize that, in time, the sun will rise and set, but not for him. If he had a tombstone, he would be pleased to have it bear Herrick's inscription: "Gather ye rosebuds while ye may."

Horace would have made a congenial traveling companion for me. My friends laugh that sometimes I stop overnight on the 260-mile trip from South Bend to Louisville. Horace would understand, for he wrote:

With inns commodious, snug and warm,
We split the journey, and perform
In two days' time what's often done
By brisker travellers in one.

Reading has something to do with an inner fitness. I heard a doctor say on television that if you want to keep your cardiovascular system fit, you need to get the heartbeat up to 120 a minute, for at least an hour, three times a week. There is a similar need for the mind and spirit. To keep them pliant, you need to put some pressure on them daily. And be concerned with the diet of the mind. Find pieces of writing that somehow strengthen you.

Since my office is in a library, I find that being surrounded by two million books is a great luxury. They bring both gratitude and sadness—gratitude for the richness and sadness for a vastness that can never be explored. So much in so little time.

While walking up Notre Dame Avenue this morning I was thinking of the libraries in Louisville, Fort Bragg, Palma and dozens of other places around the world. The search for serendipity has been a recurring theme in my life. In my seventies I march to the same drummer as at seven and at seventeen. We keep our drummers all the way.

Confucius said: "I live in a very small house, but my windows look out on a very large world." When confined by old age, so that you can no longer gallivant across creation you can still use books to look at and marvel at God's very large world.

10

Tourists and Travelers

Retired people take trips more than ever these days. Since they have time to spare they might well become travelers rather than tourists.

Odysseus, for example, was a traveler, not a tourist. When Dante asked him, in the *Divine Comedy*, why had he gone to and fro upon the earth, Odysseus replied, "To gain yet more experiences of the world and of men's faults and valor." Tourists go to and fro to gain yet more experiences of men's restaurants and shops.

Travelers stretch awareness the way tourists stretch dollars. Money cannot buy the deep experiences that Odysseus wanted; they must be earned. One way to earn them is to prepare for the inner life of the trip by reading such books as H. V. Morton's travel series and the travel writings of perceptive authors such as Emerson, Carlyle, and Waugh. They will sensitize your powers of observation, for they did not pass the dust of saints and sinners unmoved by the experience.

Tourists skim the surfaces of places, but travelers settle down, from time to time, to get the feel of a locale. A Japanese poet wrote:

Not a single thing
Have I closely observed;
My feet on life's way
Are too vigorous.

A tourist's feet tend to be too vigorous. On the first
visit to a country it is all right to travel widely to get the
lay of the land, but on later visits it is best to settle
down to allow blurred experiences to come into focus.
For example, it would be a rich experience to spend
several days reading Allen Temko's *Notre Dame of Paris*
while sitting in the garden behind the cathedral, paus-
ing now and then to go inside to observe things Temko
writes about so well. That memory would cling for a
lifetime.

Even when not on a writing assignment I try to
travel as though I were. By avoiding purposeless days
there is a chance of turning experiences into memories
that do not fade too fast. For instance, I remember clearly
a morning long ago when at dawn I went to the zoo in
Central Park to have breakfast with the keepers. Had I
not known that they were speaking of their animals I
would have thought they were describing the ailments of
their children.

Nor was I on assignment the mornings I went to the
mews at Buckingham Palace to talk with grooms, mostly
ex-jockeys. Odysseus would have been interested in
hearing of the problems that confront those wiry little
men who must keep the queen's carriage horses accustomed to commotion lest they bolt during the hoopla of
some royal occasion. On most mornings the grooms sub-

ject the horses to rush-hour traffic, and after that any pandemonium is acceptable.

One day the grooms were worried about Burmese, a gift to the queen from Canada. They had asked the queen not to ride the frisky filly in her birthday parade, but she was determined to do so. The next day at the Horse Guards Parade Grounds, Burmese was restive but did not bolt. A decade later she was a serene mare when a fanatic fired a shot during the queen's birthday ceremonials.

Unless on a writing assignment, it takes some discipline to read for a trip and even more to write about the experience without a deadline. But the way to keep travel from being aimless and help it stick in the memory is to impose some order on those fragments of happenings.

Friends ask why I don't take photographs or make sketches to illustrate my articles and books. I have never learned to take professional photographs, and even after doing graduate work in art I am less interested in sketching than in writing. Besides to do either would blur the kind of attention—and it is a very different kind—needed for the written word.

For example, it was an uneasy experience in Venice the morning I sketched the four bronze horses above the entrance to Saint Mark's Cathedral. Instead of looking at them until I really "saw" them, as one should when sketching, I allowed the mind to play with words, thinking that those statues have been seen by most of the people we read about in history. A Greek fashioned them three or four hundred years before Christ. Rome stole them to garnish the Arch of Nero. Constantine sent them to grace the towers of the hippodrome in Constantinople. Venetians sacked that city, in 1203, and shipped the horses to Venice. After the fall of the Republic in 1797, Napoleon, who could covet with the best, sent the bronzes to Paris to adorn the Arc du Carrousel. The horses were brought back to Venice in 1815 and restored to their position on the open platform above the atrium of Saint Mark's.

My sketch turned out sorry, indeed. I was giving the bronze horses the kind of attention needed for entries in a traveler's notebook, while they required a different sort of concentration for drawing.

When I fail to make notes I regret it afterward. For instance, on a train ride from Washington, D.C. to North Carolina in 1951, I met a man in the club car who designed pinball machines. He was full of talk about what makes a good pinball game and what is just a banal effort. His lecture, and it was that, made me sense that he was something of a genius in the field— a Babe Ruth or a Leonardo. If only I had written down the secrets of his successes as we rolled past red clay hills and scrub pines!

I also regret not having made notes on a conversation one night in India. Lieutenant Paul Geren and I visited three couples, all missionaries from England, in a remote part of the Punjab. When the native guides, after a long journey, finally led us into the mission compound we found the couples in evening gowns and tuxedos. Our host explained, "We dress for dinner each evening. It helps separate us from the day." That is the lone sentence

I recall, forty years later, from what must have been an interesting visit.

Whether you take photographs, draw sketches, or write in a notebook, the thing is to keep experiences alive, to avoid a life full of forgettable days. In *Working and Thinking on the Waterfront,* Eric Hoffer observed: "How easy it is to forget a mood or perhaps feelings in general. We can remember an act or something we saw, heard, or smelled, but we cannot remember the feelings of happiness, despair, elation, dejection, etc., unless we have encased them in words."

Thomas Mallon, in *A Book of One's Own,* wrote: "The telephone has more or less killed letter-writing, and the camera has dealt a pretty severe blow to the travel diary, but some energy for the latter survives. We all have the certainty of our own unique way of seeing places, a sense that the camera can be too objective a recorder of our trips away from home. We sometimes like the chance to say this is what I, not the Nikon, saw. The diary still gives that."

Here, for example, are a few entries from my travel diary. They have kept some experiences alive through the years; as I reread these sentences those days come back in some detail.

Fiji
August 23, 1980

Father Denis Fitzpatrick, the administrator of the cathedral parish here in Suva, loves to recall boyhood days in a village in County Mayo. One of his best memories is of the parish priest whose nephew was James Corbett, the heavyweight boxing champion.

The uncle would tell at great length how Gentleman Jim, on September 7, 1892, knocked out the great John L. Sullivan in the first heavyweight fight ever to use the Marquis of Queensberry rules. The betting—Glory be!—was five to one on Sullivan, the Human Pile Driver. The parish priest always ended the story: "In round twenty-one James landed a smashing right to the jaw. The champion of champions fell, as falls an oak tree, slowly, majestically."

Eventually Gentleman Jim came to visit his uncle in Ireland. He basked in the warmth of County Mayo admirers because in the States the Irish were slow to forgive him for his "crime" of toppling their hero from his heights.

Corbett was so pleased with his reception that he offered to give a demonstration of his skills against some of the strong boys of Mayo. One of them observed, "You cannot touch his head, for his neck is like rubber." The money raised from the affair, attended by most of western Ireland, was put into the parish fund.

When Corbett returned to the States his uncle had a large stone moved to the parish grounds and upon it was engraved the fact that on this spot Gentleman Jim Corbett, heavyweight champion of the whole world, fought the local lads.

At the village pub scarcely a pint was drunk without someone recalling some fact from Corbett's career: he was the fourth of twelve children, he had worked as a clerk in a San Francisco bank, and his father, Patrick, was from Ireland. And often on their way down the lane the lads stopped at the stone to recall the great day.

When Jim Corbett's career in the ring ended, he went into vaudeville and motion pictures. Eventually he got a divorce, or married a divorcée, or maybe both. It was a blow to his uncle, the parish priest in County Mayo.

The old man shook his head, got up off his knees, and went into the village to borrow mallet and chisel. And as Father Fitzpatrick tells it, "He chiseled the name of Gentleman Jim out of the stone and out of his heart."

Williamsburg
August 17, 1960

On the campus of William and Mary I came upon an old man down on his knees repairing the brick sidewalks. He is a dead ringer for Uncle Remus. I asked about a statue I had seen here two years ago; it had stood in front of Wren Hall since colonial times, if I am not mistaken.

The old man said that vandalism made it necessary to take away the statue. Somebody kept painting it. He shook his head: "There it stand a couple hundred years and now we got to take it down. Wrap it up and put it in a warehouse where nobody can touch it and nobody can see it. Why somebody have to molest it, I just don't know. Seem they would see that's like something sacred. But no! I just don't know why it have to be."

He pointed across the lawn to a cannon that had been used in the Revolution. About every other year somebody hauls it away. The last time it was found deep in a ravine in the woods.

He kept shaking his head: "Why do it have to be?"

The old man said that the loss of regard for tradition goes beyond the student body. He told of a man who had been a tradition here; he had rung the bells every day for more than fifty years. When he retired the administration installed an electric bell-ringing system.

The bricklayer returned to his chipping, and just when I thought he had forgotten about me, and I was about to leave, he pointed to a plaque near the college entrance. He said that he had mounted that plaque and while mounting it he had thought a good deal about something it says. The plaque tells that the college was founded through a charter granted by King William and Queen Mary in 1693 for "educating the young in good letters and manners."

"What has happened to manners?" the old man asked as though expecting no answer.

Cagayan de Oro
Mindanao
November 10, 1976

Father Fahey told me about an experience he had as a boy in Ireland, one that has haunted him ever since. In a pub, near the edge of a lake, a deeply-disturbed half-drunk said to him:

"Lad, let me tell you something. I have fought for old Ireland. I killed my best friend for Ireland. What did it get me! I'm over there with John Bull, down in the mines, with my cap in my hand, and glad to get it."

During the fighting in 1918, he explained, his best friend was suspected of spying for the British. His commanding officer ordered him to invite his friend fishing and shoot him. So he did. In the middle of the lake he shot him and threw the body overboard.

So now he works in England. Sends money to his wife every week. He comes home once a year to visit her. And to stand by the lake.

New York Harbor
The Queen Elizabeth
August 1, 1956

Just before sailing things were really confused aboard ship, a turmoil caused by many visitors. They filled all available space with noise and tilted champagne glasses. So much picture-taking was going on that it was impossible to take a step along the deck without ruining someone's shot.

The average passenger must be at least 60. Some are in the December of life and many in late November. Age makes no difference; you can be a tourist as long as you breathe a little every day.

There seems to be a new breed of professional tourists. They travel about waiting for life to run out, while speaking about the *Mauretania*, Swissair, and the Blue Mosque.

They will multiply as long as money is plentiful, and retirement age is 65, and life's span lengthens. In time herds of aged nomads will drift back and forth

between Lake Louise and Lake Como, and trek up
and down from Nassau to the hills of Darjeeling.

Just as chaos on all the decks had built to a cli-
max, a steward went about beating a Chinese gong
and shouting "All ashore who's going ashore!"

The visitors left with reluctance and lined the
pier to wave goodbye. As the ship began to move, a
woman on shore shouted to a woman aboard, "Don't
get mixed up with any schoolteacher, grab a guy with
money!"

As Thomas Mallon said, " . . . this is what I, not the
Nikon, saw." And besides if you write things down you
are not apt to return home like the elderly woman who
could not recall Venice. Her daughter helped by saying,
"But, Momma, don't you remember the place we bought
the five-button gloves?"

Writing usually opens you to your surroundings.
The tourist travels in a shell of his own environment, and,
since little pierces it, returns home unchanged. The traveler, open to unfamiliar ways, respects but does not always enjoy the manners and values of other countries.

Aldous Huxley told of a simple game he played to
open himself to his milieu. While traveling one of his
great delights was to sit in a cafe, restaurant, or aboard a
train looking at people and, without attempting to enter
into the conversation, collect scraps of their talk: "From
their appearance, from what they say, one constructs in
the imagination the whole character, the complete life
history. Given the single fossil bone, one fancifully builds
up the whole diplodocus. It is an excellent game. But it
must be played discreetly." Huxley warned that too open

a curiosity is apt to be resented. You must look and listen without appearing to be aware of anything.

When something goes wrong on a trip, if you write about it the pain is somewhat lessened. I hope that the character in Flaubert's novel, *Sentimental Journey,* was keeping a traveler's notebook: "He traveled. He knew the melancholy of the steamboat; the cold awakening in the tent; the tedium of scenery and ruins; the bitterness of interrupted friendship." It has been forever so.

But Flaubert's character did not have to endure jet lag which comes when inner clocks are disrupted by crashing through several time zones. I envy those who do not suffer too much from it. My inner mechanism is set for steamboats and stagecoaches.

Cicadian dysrhythmia, the medical term for jet lag, always seemed most severe when flying eastward. I thought that was my imagination until United Airlines published an article saying that eastward more than westward flights reduce mental sharpness and bring on indigestion and headaches.

On a trans-Pacific flight a doctor told me that after crashing through time zones some tourists visit his office in Honolulu complaining that they are coming down with something. They feel washed out, as though the bottom has dropped out of their blood pressure; they sense the uneasiness that comes during recovery from an illness.

Since our inner clocks bring us good days and bad days, physically and psychologically, woe be unto those whose jet lag coincides with the bad days. That, like lost baggage, gets a trip off to an uneasy start.

Suffering from *cicadian dysrhythmia* is less disturbing, though, than suffering from the vulgarization of things. It used to be that only tourists got entangled in the vulgarities of a place; a traveler had enough sophistication to know how to avoid them. Avoidance is no longer possible. There is no escape; the exits have all been locked. Go by train, plane, boat or car and you will find the destroyers waiting.

The great blight of the world comes from a lack of reverence. Rich soil, clear water and pure air are ruined by a spiritual deficiency, a shortage of appreciation. This comes from a want of sense and sensitivity, coupled with selfishness galore.

The blight has emptied our cities of significance. They go through the same paces that they always did, but the importance has gone out of them. This is especially tragic for places that were once great. A terrible greyness smothers the cities. They lack zest despite gaudy graffiti and shattering decibels. The approaches to our cities, chaotic with rampant hype, are turbulent with flaunting signs and the commotion of shabby merchandising. Poverty did not cause such ugliness; affluence did. Since all of that money bought junk instead of beauty, it must have been spent by a culture flabby and tasteless.

I used to blame automobiles for the ruin of cities. How wonderful it would have been to walk in Rome before the coming of the automobile, I thought, and then came across a disillusioning passage that Juvenal wrote about Rome at the end of the first century:

> Here many invalids die from being kept awake.
> Where can you find lodgings that give you a chance

of sleeping? In the city, sleep is luxury that costs a
fortune. This is the prime cause of illness. The roar
of the wheeled traffic in the city's narrow winding
streets and the shouts of abuse are enough to rob us
of sleep.

By coincidence, the day I read Juvenal's complaints
I came upon a magazine article saying that Dr. Vern O.
Knudsen, of the University of California, found that ex-
posure to over ninety decibels can flush the skin, con-
strict the stomach muscles, and shorten tempers. Other
doctors, the article said, suspect that noise may be a hidden factor in heart disease, high blood pressure, allergy,
nervousness and even mental health.

Vulgarization now shows in many new ways. Turn on
a radio, for instance, in almost any part of the world and
little of what you hear will sound civilized, because the
immature of all countries copy the worst that America has
to offer. When General Grant visited Japan he gave the
emperor good advice which has been ignored: "Take the
best of western civilization and leave the rest."

BBC broadcasts used to be so good that I often spent
too much time while in England listening to the radio.
About a decade ago someone at the BBC took a national
survey to find out what the people want. That did it.

England used to be a country of courtesy and good
manners. Eric Hoffer said, "A revulsion for work has
swept Britain in the past two decades." With that revulsion came the loss of civility. British Railways, aware of
the decline, is starting a "civility course" for employees.
I remember an elegant English lady on a train to Corn-

wall who when subjected to rudeness said, "And to think we fought a war for this."

Another English woman said, "When everyone travels it will be very nice to stay at home."

So much of life is crowd-ridden. Crowds fill airports, hotel lobbies, restaurants, and highways. Everyone is in motion, but not getting anywhere. When individuals are turned into crowd-people, standards slip and gimmicks and fads thrive. Quality becomes of little concern.

Barbarism infects crowds. Just look at the depth of litter on a college campus after a football game. There is a certain ruthlessness about crowds, even friendly ones.

Nine hundred years ago in the churches of Europe some Catholics prayed: "From the Viking terror, Lord, deliver us." We need such a prayer today begging for deliverance from destroyers already inside the grounds. They have the spirit of Genghis Khan's horsemen whose battle cry was: "Where we ride the grass will never grow again!"

The two best things about travel are looking forward to a trip and getting home again. Since looking forward is rewarding, it is well to book the trip two months or more ahead of departure. In that way when something in life goes haywire, you can shrug it off with, "Oh well, five weeks from today I'll be in Vienna!"

Upon returning home you are glad to settle into the old routine, pleased with your lot in life. For the time being you have suffered enough of what Hamlet called, "the thousand natural shocks that flesh is heir to." Of course the feeling of well-being, now wrapped around you, will wear thin in time. Then you will take another trip.

11

Time to Remember

My grandfather's walking stick I value, but I would cherish even more a few hundred pages of his life's story. A journal or a memoir would be a wonderful heirloom, especially if it told what he had learned about life from having lived it. No two people can reach identical conclusions about that, and if they do one is copying the answers.

Journals and memoirs are valued by future generations, but they can also be helpful here and now. Such writing helps keep the Greek admonition: Know thyself. For instance, it checks the quality of your activity. In putting on paper a list of things you have been doing you may come to wonder if they are worth doing. You may also discover things left undone. In Matthew 15 men are condemned not for anything done, but for six things left undone.

Whether or not you ever take pen in hand, by middle age you have written a script about yourself, figuratively speaking, and your friends have reviewed your show long ago. The problem is for you to hear the *real you* delivering the lines and coming in on cue. Words put onto paper over a long time might help you catch yourself in your act.

Rereading a journal is like coming upon a wall where

in youth you stood from time to time to chalk your height. Or it is like finding an old family album. How you changed, and you hadn't noticed!

At seventy-five an Englishman reread his diaries and said: "I find that they are all about a person I recognize, but also about a man who went away a long time ago to leave room for the present one."

Since everything is changing—the universe, the apple tree and you—a journal helps give a glimpse of what you are becoming. The devil in *Screwtape Letters* says, "All mortals tend to turn into the thing they are pretending to be."

In Eliot's poem, *East Coker*, is the line: "Old men ought to be explorers." Exploring the inner self is an adventure that might go on to the very end. The exploration is never complete, as the diaries of Gide, at eighty, and Berenson, at ninety, prove. Some people quit exploring at an early age; it is too much trouble to keep it up. Meditation and contemplation are hard, and when they are carried on through a journal they are doubly difficult because writing is difficult.

When a journal records an inward journey of exploration, what emerges is a landscape of sorts with its moral horizons and spiritual atmosphere, call it the terrain of the soul. If you want to observe the terrain of three very different souls, read the journals of Anne Morrow Lindberg, Virginia Woolf and Anais Nin.

In every person there are vast unexplored tracts, misty boundaries which can be pushed back by writing. Writing hauls to the surface thoughts you did not know were there, and encourages shaping those blurred notions and hunches into ideas you may be willing to stand behind. It helps to turn your inner chaos into something of a cosmos.

A journal can help you find a pattern in your life—call it a theme, a recurring motif. But years must accumulate before this happens. It is like working a jigsaw puzzle: when you have only a few pieces the picture looks spotty, but when many pieces are in place—call them life's experiences—a design emerges. To put it another way, in old age with the help of a journal you stand on a mountain overlooking a vast prospect. Fields, hills, valleys and streams seem to fit together.

If judged by the days, life does not make much sense. Judged by the years, things add up and a plan emerges. A good reason to write a memoir is to have the satisfaction—call it the consolation—of seeing patterns form. John Muir, the naturalist, observed: "Whenever I tried to separate anything out by itself, I found it hitched to something else in the universe." What a consolation that insight is!

A journal also helps you realize that life is a carousel. Katherine Anne Porter wrote to her nephew: "Each generation must get on the same merry-go-round, only disguised in a fresh coat of paint." In old age Harry Truman felt compelled to repeat that the only thing new in the world is the history you don't know. Thomas Merton said that looking back in his journal he was surprised to find that an observation he had written this morning, thinking it was fresh, he found he had written five years earlier.

Mark Harris has kept a diary every day since January 1, 1934. In 1977 he wrote: "It is a record of every place I have been every day, of everyone I have known. It is a tracing of my journey through the world. Granted a certain egotistical perversity to it, nevertheless I wouldn't feel normal going to bed without recording my day. My diary has stabilized me, offering me perspective. It has helped me to see, by looking back, life's cyclic shape so that I was able to understand, when at last I heard it, the advice of poet Robert Frost not to let anything get me too far up or too far down."

This suggests that keeping a journal can be a form of therapy. It seemed therapeutic for André Gide who said, "I did well to write those lines yesterday. It purged me. This evening I feel quite reconciled with the universe and with myself."

Anais Nin wrote: "If you cannot control your demons, whoever or whatever they are, you do harm to others. I found the way to cage mine, that was all. Anger, jealousy, envy, revengefulness, vanity: I locked them up in a diary."

Saint Augustine used writing to unburden his conscience. Emerson said that no matter how disheveled the day, all disasters seem less painful in the evening once they are recorded. When Dag Hammarskjold began keeping a journal he called it "a sort of white book concerning my negotiations with myself—and with God."

Keeping a journal can be a form of worship. That is because it is easier to believe in the providence of God once life reveals a pattern. As long as you think that chance rules the day, you can't very well stand in awe of providence.

In an article in *Review for Religious*, Father Edward

J. Farrell told of his prayer journal: "One of the ways I have learned to pray is by writing. I began by copying favorite passages from reading, then thoughts and ideas of others, and finally came to jotting down my own insights and reflections from the prayer and experiences of each day."

When I was in Korea writing the biography of Archbishop Harold Henry, he said, at age sixty-five, that working on the manuscript was the best spiritual retreat he had ever made. By going back over the years in great detail, taking inventory, he became aware of how God can break into ordinary lives in new and startling ways.

If you are one of those people who would rather talk on a telephone than write letters, you might prefer to put your thoughts on tape. Videotape would be even better. If someone interviewed you, drew you out, you might give more detail and be more definite about the life you have lived.

Whenever I urge people to keep journals or write memoirs the usual response is, "Who would care?" A more truthful response would be, "It's too much trouble!" Yes, it is trouble. Writing is an onerous business.

A boyhood friend, Joseph Steltenpohl, wrote interesting letters home during the Second World War. Lately he had them published in book form, bringing back to us details long forgotten. At about the same time, another friend, Professor Elizabeth Christman, had her father's wartime letters published. She observed that his grandchildren were even more delighted with the heirloom than his children. My guess is that the great-grandchildren will be even more so. Another friend, Father

Gerald Lardner, gave me a copy of the memoir his father had written during the last ten months of life. Although I never met Michael Lardner, I found his book, *Keep the Fair Side Out*, delightful to read.

Anyone completing a memoir should give copies to all relatives, especially to children and grandchildren, to local and state historical societies, and to college archives. I am very aware that religious ought to write for their community's archives, for while doing research in such archives in Ireland I was often thankful to someone long-dead for having put experiences onto paper.

Things become hallowed with time—Roman coins, Greek vases, paintings in a cave in France. During the centenary of the Civil War, diaries of private soldiers came out in book form, words that no publisher would have found publishable a hundred years earlier.

As for your journal's value to posterity, I don't mean that you ought to seek applause from descendants. No use courting an admiration you will not live to enjoy. But if what you write today gives someone pleasure after you are gone, that is as worth doing as giving pleasure in the here and now.

If you don't want to keep a journal, perhaps you might keep a commonplace book. It would also have some psychological value because it will give you something to point to.

A steelworker, Mike Lefevre, said that he would like to see as part of every building a foot-wide metal strip from top to bottom. On it would be listed the name of each bricklayer, electrician, carpenter and welder who had worked on the construction.

"So when a guy walked by he could say to his son, 'See, that's me over there on the forty-fifth floor. I put the beam in.' Picasso can point to a painting. A writer can point to a book. What can I point to? Everybody should have something to point to."

William Faulkner believed that what keeps a writer writing is a need to leave some mark on life. He observed that everybody has the urge to scrawl, "Kilroy was here."

Years ago an old actor expressed dismay at the impermanence of his art: "Every night I carve a statue in a block of ice."

The actor, and Faulkner, and Mike Lefevre were aware that so much of what we do is ephemeral and that we need something enduring to point to.

If you sense such a need, especially in old age, you might ease it by keeping a commonplace book in which you copy whatever strikes you. The entries in your book—aphorisms, poems, bits of conversations—may vary in length from one sentence to several paragraphs.

The important thing is that you respond to the ideas in it. You might, at times, write your reaction beneath them. In *A Commonplace Book,* by Charles P. Curtis, the author used each quote as a starting point for an editorial journey. On the other hand, W.H. Auden said in the introduction to *A Certain World:* "I have tried to keep my own reflections to a minimum and let others, more learned, intelligent, imaginative and witty than I, speak for me."

When young I never took notes while reading unless, of course, an exam loomed up ahead. Now I believe more in the Aristotelian idea that whatever is expressed is impressed: Talking out an idea impresses it upon you, but writing it out impresses it still more.

I read with pencil in hand. If I make no notes within the first twenty pages, the chances are the book goes right back to the shelf.

Most notes reflect a kindred spirit. They are about something I have long felt but never expressed. In a flash of recognition I say, "That's it!" When words strike a chord inside, they give off a resonance, the dial tone of the soul.

When I came upon that sentence that Simone Weil wrote, in *Waiting for God*, about the unusualness of a vocation I just had to write it down. Her observation, as you have noticed, has been a recurring theme in these pages.

I know how the shipwrecked Greek felt when, upon landing on the beach of an unknown island, he looked at footprints in the sand and exclaimed, "So we are home here!" That is the thrill I get when sensing the presence of another human being in a perceptive sentence.

What you copy down tells much about you and is almost as revealing as your journal. A commonplace book may seem like an easy alternative to a journal, but it is not. To find sentences worth recording, you have to read things more substantial than newspapers.

While keeping a commonplace book you are more alert in your reading, just as when keeping a journal you live with more awareness. Such disciplines are part of the struggle against a closed-in, droning existence.

Saint Irenaeus said: "The glory of God is man fully alive."

In the sixteenth century Blaise de Montluc was under siege at Siena. His troops were weak with exhaustion, starving and outnumbered. He said: "So, in the mornings, before I showed myself to them, I would slap my face with wine, until I looked as young and fresh as when I was a lover in the Piedmont."

Pasternak said of a certain poet: "If he had really suffered he might have written the major work of which he is capable." Ernst Barlack said something similar to a friend: "I once remarked to you that there is a law that no work can turn out successfully unless it goes through a severe crisis that deepens and spiritualizes it."

André Malraux asked a priest what he had learned while hearing confessions for the past fifteen years. The priest answered, "People are much more unhappy than one thinks. And then there's no such thing as a grown-up person."

A Chinese philosopher in the fifth century said: "I gratify my spirit and nothing more. What is there that is more important than gratifying my spirit?"

Something copied may influence what you think and

write and say. In 1945 John F. Kennedy wrote in his commonplace book a quotation from Rousseau: "As soon as
any man says of the affairs of state, What does it matter
to me? the state may be given up as lost." Sixteen years
later he said in his inaugural address: "And so, my fellow
Americans, ask not what your country can do for you; ask
what you can do for your country."

Here are some of the notes I have made in recent
weeks. Nearly every one is an echo of something I have
been saying in this book. Many of my jottings run several
paragraphs, but here, for the sake of brevity, I will use
only short ones:

In the Talmud is written: "It is not your ob-
ligation to complete your work, but you are not
at liberty to quit."

Toward the end of his life when James Joyce was
asked what he had retained of his Jesuit education he replied: "To arrange things so that
they can be grasped and judged."

A Swedish proverb says: "The old man shows
what the young man was."

In 514 B.C., Lao Tzu wrote: "To realize that our
knowledge is ignorance, that is a noble insight."

Before she was fifteen, Anne Frank wrote in her

diary: "I have had a lot of sorrow, but who hasn't at my age."

The Chinese have a proverb: "That the birds of worry and care fly above your head, this you cannot change. But that they build nests in your hair, this you can prevent."

Teresa of Avila, that wise nun, said: "It is when I possess least that I have fewest worries. I am more afflicted when there is excess of anything than when there is a lack of it."

In a letter to the BBC, a listener complained about people who say on the air: "Have a good day" or "Have a nice weekend." He said, "The BBC doesn't give a hoot whether or not I have a good day. Sincere formality is far better than hollow good cheer."

On a train from Dublin to Killiney I heard a schoolboy ask another, "Do you like geography?" and the reply was, "No, you learn too much about a place."

"Knowledge is the source of all mystery," said Shen-hui.

In his notebook Gogol wrote: "It is sad not to
see the good in goodness."

Taking notes is like planting seeds—some germinate and
some don't. At the time you plant you never know which
will and which will not. You at times wonder whatever
attracted you to some of the notes that you have taken.

Every man seeks the thing which he uniquely has to
say, observed Jean Guitton, and added, "He seeks the
secret of his self which he cannot see because he carries
it on his back."

A notebook helps you say the things you need to say,
and might give you a glimpse of the secret you carry on
your back. A woman, living alone in a London flat, at
eighty-two, sensed this when she wrote: "A notebook
might be the very thing for all the old who wave away
crossword puzzles, painting, petit point, and knitting. It
is more restful than conversation, and for me it has become a companion, more, a confessional. It cannot shrive
me, but knowing myself better comes near to that."

As I said earlier, a doctor observed that if you want
to keep your cardiovascular system fit, you need to get
your heartbeat up to 120 a minute, for at least an hour,
three times a week. There is a like need for mind and
spirit; if you want to keep them pliant, you will need to
put some pressure on them daily. And be concerned with
the diet of the mind, by finding pieces of writing that
somehow strengthen you. It won't be easy; there is not
much of that going around.

As the steelworker, Mike Lefevre, said, "Everybody should have something to point to." Everyone feels the need to make a mark on this three-dimensional world. Your diary and commonplace book are worth pointing to, and they will have value long after you are beyond the reach of injurious time. As heirlooms they will be treasured. They are worth cherishing more than things that end up at a garage sale.

12

Lord, Give Me Patience
—NOW!

A fey fellow described a friend as having the look of a harassed stork. An old man in County Wicklow had just such a look. Eighty and bedridden, he used to wheeze with annoyance, "This tag-end of life is a hellish trial on my patience."

Impatience was alienating him from those who were a happy part of his past. As a Chinese philosopher said: "A moment of patience may ward off a disaster, and a moment of impatience may ruin a life."

The old Irishman needed a sign above his bed similar to the one at the entrance to a small London park: COMMIT NO NUISANCE. Such admonition might well be nailed above the gateway to the universe.

In lashing out, the Wicklow octogenarian joins a crowded company, according to a doctor who spends much time with the elderly. Those who cannot accept their lot are bitter, cantankerous and demanding, he said: "Their feeling and thinking are narrowed down to a small circle, in the center of which they sit in their wheelchairs, thoroughly nasty old people with few or no saving graces."

Acceptance is unpopular in our time. "Fight back"

is the motto. Assertiveness training is very big. You are supposed to feel sorry for yourself and punch the nose of anybody who fails to share in your attitude.

Some restless spirits seem to enjoy disenchantment. They act as though a dreary disposition is required by law, and they guard the pursuit of moroseness as an inalienable right, like the pursuit of happiness. If they show much agitation on the surface, they probably lack sensitivity in the depths.

I knew a man, still young, who took delight in feeling sorry for himself. While performing his act in the presence of a Jesuit, the priest exclaimed, "Oh, Hank, you are a third century Christian!"

"What do you mean by that?"

"In the third century the Christians were no longer persecuted, but they wanted to be."

An elderly widow in our neighborhood collects complaints the way small boys collect baseball cards. She seems to have everything going for her—a comfortable home, no responsibilities, good health, sufficient income—and yet she has a grievance for every season. I asked a friend, advanced in age and wisdom, why she acts that way. He said that since everybody needs some drama in life, and since the widow lacks it, she goes ahead and creates it, and that gives her something to live for.

The people who think it is their right to be tyrannical enjoy it as their last emotional pleasure. When trapped by the tyranny of the weak, the strong feel guilty about their own resentments. Nietzsche complained that Christianity gives the weak too much power over the strong. A Christianity that stresses sentimentality certainly does that.

If old age requires you to depend on others, as it did to the man in Wicklow Town, it is well not to call attention to your plight. Go ahead and share in the unspoken sorrow of the world. Besides, when dependency is caused by nature it does no good to lash out. Nature needs to be appeased.

I saw the wisdom of such appeasement among the Kachins in upper Burma. When nature confronts them, instead of fighting back, they respond in a natural way. For instance, they plant millet at the edge of all fields because birds prefer it to other grains; they plant sesame throughout the fields knowing insects will gorge themselves on it. And so the crops are spared.

Such appeasement is a form of acceptance. It reflects humility, patience, wisdom, those graces the old man in County Wicklow lacked. He needed the disposition of a certain elderly veteran of the First World War living in rural England. When a social worker apologized to him for not being able to provide fuel to heat his damp, cold cottage, he said: "Don't worry. Sixty-two years ago today I was in the trenches. Mud and water up to my hips. This is better."

That old veteran is like Job, after learning his lesson. When Job complained, God said: "Where were you when I laid the foundations of the earth?" Job got the point. Seeing in a flash the inexpressible omnipotence of God, he said: "Behold, I am of small account; what shall I answer thee? I lay my hand on my mouth."

Such acceptance and patience comes from new-found humility. Until then it is easy to speak of putting trust in God while acting as though God can't be trusted, easy to grow bitter over the prayer unanswered and the disaster undeserved, seeing God as a spoilsport. Until Job found humility he might well have painted the sign: "Lord, give me patience—NOW!"

When the body becomes dry and brittle, like a leaf at year's end, and the mind lacks the energy to grasp new things, that is when you really need patience. That virtue, always hard to come by, is especially evasive if death eludes you when you are "full of years." If the tag-end of life brings the indignity of helplessness, to be sentenced to life can be as dreadful as being sentenced to death. Even to speak of such a condition takes courage. One must be terribly brave to get through life in an admirable way. That is why it lifted the heart to hear an elderly nun say to young novices: "When you are old you won't be able to see anymore. Now all I can see is God. And God sees me; that's enough."

Virtues ought to be less elusive when you reach the time of life when it is no longer safe to experiment with them. And some are more readily courted by then, but not all—especially not that of patience.

As control slips away, patience can bring some sense of control. As Christ says in the Gospel of Luke: "In your patience you shall possess your souls." The concordance of Scriptures gives *patience* a lengthy listing—less than that of peace but equal to that of perfection. In most books of spiritual direction patience gets a good press.

Patience is a part of charity. When Saint Paul was trying to describe what he meant by charity, he said it "endureth all things," and went on to observe that it is even more important than faith and hope. The inability to endure all things shows a lack of faith and hope, for faith and hope are flawed unless there is an unreserved acceptance. Real faith does not believe in God by halves. Acceptance, filled with hope, makes one's life something of a work of art by giving it unity and by driving out the banality of the complainer.

Patience is a virtue worth cultivating for selfish reasons if for no other. Patient people seem to have a better time of it than do the irascible. The main day-to-day value is that patience lightens burdens beyond avoiding.

Burdens beyond avoiding are many, and no way of life guarantees one hundred percent relief from them. Since the rain falls alike on the just and the unjust it is not just drenching you. Everyone you meet is carrying a heavy burden, or has been, or soon will be. If you have been paying attention to the ways of the world you have a feeling for what Gibbon called "the vicissitudes of fortune, which spares neither man nor the proudest of his works, which buries empires and cities in a common grave." If you still think it is possible to be completely separated from frustrations and misery, you are unlearned in the ABC's of life. Bureaucrats speak of "hardship cases," but everybody is filed under that category more or less. It takes maturity to say, "Well, yes, pain is a part of being human and I am so very human."

Sometimes you gain a new freedom by letting loose of the powers of the past which sets limits on your life. The gymnast, for instance, practices for six hours a day getting ready for the Olympics, but in so doing limits development in other ways. When, in time, the athletic skill decreases, the gymnast can accept this as a chance to develop in ways there was no time for in the past.

In retirement there is the danger that life will become such a backwater it will turn brackish. One needs to go forward in another direction, perhaps an even more adventurous one.

Even confinement can have value. When Ignatius of Loyola had to stay in bed for several months to recover from battle wounds suffered in the siege of Pamplona, he had time to read and to think. The experience changed him from "one of the boys" to one of the world's great moral educators.

The greatest freedom, that of the spirit, requires a certain submissiveness, a submissiveness to grace. There is something "graceful" about abandoning the things of life before death comes along to do the job for you. The things worth acquiring in old age are those the government cannot tax—patience, acceptance, humility, courage. You do that by making a separate peace with life, "a unilateral agreement," as they say at the conference table.

Ill health puts acceptance to its greatest test. In one of her letters George Eliot wrote, "The highest calling and election is to bear pain with clear-eyed endurance." The tendency is to lash out with, "Why me?" It takes admirable character not to feel dejected over the loss of old powers but to go ahead and create some kind of life with whatever time is available.

Humility accepts suffering. Not false humility which is a part of sentimentality. The real thing never loses the sense of self-worth. Suffering accepted is a form of strength. The Scandinavians have a saying, "The north wind made the Vikings."

The privations of old age are not so damaging as the inability to take them in stride. If you don't accept them, chances are you will try to hide away in a neurosis. Then you may spend many years and much money having an analyst help you dig yourself out. Not to be able to accept things causes the spirit to harden even before the arteries do.

Not to receive old age with grace means that the inner life is not unfolding properly, and that is an immaturity. To say that someone is immature at seventy sounds silly, but that can happen. An elderly adolescent is a grotesquery.

You will never get a good grade in maturity until you accept the conditions reality imposes on you. If you reach the stage when you are not merely resigned to events but even enjoy and appreciate the force of circumstance, you may graduate summa cum laude. When you appreciate the script that providence has handed you, you are in harmony with life. This is as close to joy as you are apt to come. And as Saint Augustine said, "It doth make a difference from whence cometh a man's joy." If joy seems out of your league, you might at least try feeling fortunate.

Old age is often seen as something to be endured—a buzz, a blur, a vague sadness—even as a nightmare full of horror that destroys body and soul. Jung, however, took a more accepting view: "A human being would certainly not grow to be seventy or eighty years old if longevity had no meaning for the species. This afternoon of life must have a significance of its own and cannot be merely a pitiful appendage of life's morning."

I suppose he is saying that in the plan of God nothing is purposeless. Nature is not capricious; it only seems that way when we don't know enough about it. If we really saw creation as a whole we would recognize the inevitability of each breeze, leaf, and snowflake.

You, too, are not without purpose no matter how ancient you become. To be alive means that you still have a part to play in the magnificent drama. You are still needed, if God, like great artists, creates with an economy of means. The script contains what is needed, no more and no less. The ancient Greeks said that an excellent piece of creative work is such that nothing can be rightly added or rightly taken away. Marcus Aurelius said, "Nothing will happen to me which is not conformable to the nature of the Universe."

The distraught old man in Wicklow should have learned that in the economy of God there are no leftovers. He would not still be around if his presence on this blue planet had no purpose.

Cardinal Newman was aware of this when in *Meditations and Devotions* he wrote:

> God has created me to do him some definite service; he has committed some work to me which he has not committed to another. . . .
> Therefore I trust him. Whatever, wherever I am, I can never be thrown away. If I am in sickness, my sickness may serve him; in perplexity, my per-

plexity may serve him. My sickness, or perplexity, or sorrow may be necessary causes of some great end, which is quite beyond us.

He does nothing in vain; he may prolong my life, he may shorten it; he knows what he is about. He may take away my friends, he may throw me among strangers, he may make me feel desolate, make my spirits sink, hide the future from me—still he knows what he is about.

If only the old man in Wicklow could follow King Lear who, learning from his diminishments, turned from shallowness to wisdom. Such conversions are more apt to happen in fiction than in fact, for what a man is in his middle years he is apt to be at the end. Life is of such a piece that his values and his reactions to all experiences will shape his latter days.

Plato knew that. When he was nearing death a friend of his asked how to live wisely, and the philosopher answered, "Practice dying." The way to practice dying is to live life with the awareness that Cardinal Newman spoke of. To live life as a vocation, as he saw it, brings deep satisfaction and is a way of letting God into the world.

To see God working out his purposes when things go your way is easy, but to see such purposes unfolding when things go contrary to your wishes takes faith. Like every act of faith it is a leap into the dark.

Acceptance is not the same as resignation, at least not as I use it. Acceptance is affirmative, even joyful, but resignation is negative, even disgruntled. Accepting old age does not mean a grudging, "Oh well, all right." It means "Yes!" with a ring of gratitude in it, a form of worship. Suggesting that old age be accepted with gratitude may sound strange—it has had such a bad press—but if it is part of God's plan what else can you do?

To refuse to accept limits, trying to transcend the possible, is being out of touch with reality. Accepting what is inevitable is only common sense. Failing this, you lack the dignity proper to a human being.

A French gentleman, finding it hard to accept retirement, said, "Nothing is worse for a man than to lose his panache!" An admirable acceptance restores a certain panache, for there is something about it that is, at once, social, spiritual and aesthetic. It confers dignity, style, and grace in a way that self-pity and bitterness cannot.

In some rare human beings disease and pain bring out a radiant spirit. They have the characteristics of aloe, an Oriental wood, which when diseased develops a texture that leads to something beautiful: In the fire it smells of the high forests, a marvelous aroma. The spirits of some old people give off an incense that pleases all who come near.

I saw examples of this while on a writing assignment in the Philippines. In some remote parts I came upon a kind of acceptance that was admirable. A missionary said that when things get really severe many Filipinos say, *"Pagbuat Sa Dios"*—It is God's will. "This is not a fatalistic acceptance," he explained. "It means, 'God knows best. I don't understand, but I trust him.'"

While growing up on a farm in Kentucky I knew an old man blessed with such grace. Everybody called him Uncle Dick, and I still don't know his full name. He had the rich mahogany complexion of a well-preserved saddle, frizzy white hair, and a way of walking that suggested his feet hurt.

Uncle Dick and I were shelling corn in a barn on one of those days that people down there called "mighty searchin'," a day when damp chill searches the crevices of the soul. Suddenly a young farmhand, a shade darker than Uncle Dick, lurched through the barn doorway beating his hat against his leg to shake off the rain.

"Good mornin'," said Uncle Dick.

"What's good about it? Good for ducks!"

The old man pointed a finger and said, "It's good for ducks, and for me, and for Edward here, and for you, too, boy! It's good for everybody. This is a day that God has made."

I was too young to observe how Uncle Dick accepted old age, but he must have done so admirably, for when acceptance is found in one area of life it usually permeates others. It has a way of driving out self-pity and other nasty defects that accompany the decline of physical powers.

To see every season as more or less hard is not dark-spirited, for that is the way things are. After facing up to that, it is best to welcome with gratitude each passing clemency, in weather and in personal life. Triumph over hardships comes not through opulence or frivolity, but through accepting any destiny handed you.

In old age be satisfied with just *feeling* the truth; it is youth that wants to *see* it and *prove* it. No matter how long you exist there will always be a great many things waiting to be understood. Much will be mystery. Patience and acceptance may help penetrate some of the darkness, at least far enough to see that the most commonplace things of life are truly extraordinary. You may then rise to the divine without turning away from the earth. In *The Dangling Man,* Saul Bellow wrote, "To him, judgment is second to wonder." Those who let judgment crowd out wonder are somewhat deprived, and may find acceptance hard to come by.

13

Sing Few Sad Songs

With all seriousness an old English gentleman used to say, "Well, I think God was quite right about that." His attitude, although presented in an amusing way, is one I have found in people I consider wise.

The saints, although of varied personalities, shared his attitude. From Ignatius, the soldier, to Teresa, the nun, they were all able to say, "Amen—so be it." A devout rabbi, Hillel, said long ago, "If only once in life I could say Amen as I ought to say it, I would be satisfied."

Such an attitude reflects a kind of innocence that is possible to have even at ninety. You may know all about war, sex, and the dark side of the soul and still keep a sense of innocence, enjoying hope and avoiding bitterness, as long as you say Amen.

I have met some wise people along the way, but have noticed that some sagacity is often posthumous, existing only in the imaginative memory of those who thought they knew a wise soul but really didn't. Wisdom is not rampant and the paths are not crowded with sages. If it is true what the Talmud says, "The old who are not wise should not be called venerable," then the category of venerability is somewhat limited. Old age does not necessarily confer wisdom, even though character is best revealed late in life.

Paul Tournier, a psychologist, made this observation when dividing the elderly into two categories: "There are wonderful old people, kind, sociable, radiant with peace. Troubles and difficulties only seem to make them grow still further in serenity. They make no claims, and it is a pleasure to see them and help them. They are grateful and even astonished that things are done for them, and that they are still loved.

"And then there are awful old people, selfish, demanding, domineering, bitter. They are always grumbling and criticizing everybody. If you go to see them, they upbraid you for not having come sooner; they misjudge your best intentions, and the conversation becomes a painful conflict."

For selfish reasons, if for no other, it pays to be one of the delightful old souls. What you send out into the universe is what comes bouncing back; if you hurt others, you get hurt in return. It is something like the law of the pendulum. When you broadcast negative vibrations you are, in time, overwhelmed by them. You get what you deserve.

One reason that wisdom is not rampant among the elderly is that many of them are angry. Some, having failed to achieve their ambitions, blame others for it. All of their problems, they feel, are "out there"—the boss, the spouse, "society"—but most problems are really inside themselves. A Jesuit showed some hint of wisdom when he put a sign on his mirror: "This is the person who must be responsible for your happiness."

There are also the self-haters who turn inward to blame themselves and, in turn, suffer deep depression.

They expected things from the world which it could not give; their talents and inclinations made their hopes unrealistic.

Wisdom is a moral quality revealed more by actions than by words. It reflects the soul more than the mind, showing character through the way life is lived rather than through attainments of the intellect. Quite humble people may attain wisdom while scholars might miss it by a country mile. Logging hours in a classroom does not guarantee common sense, the foundation of wisdom. It is possible to accumulate academic credits galore and still be foolish. It happens all the time.

Common sense puts you in touch with some reality. It helps you recognize, for instance, a blind alley when you see one, and saves you from bumping your head against the same wall again and again. Alice James, the sister of William, the psychologist, and Henry, the novelist, wrote in her diary at age forty-two, "Every hour I live I become an intenser devotee to common sense!" She was en route to wisdom.

Common sense is shaped by all you have experienced and learned. Some people, though, neither experience nor learn. They file things in the convolutions of the brain to stagnate there, unhelpful and inert.

One of the things you sense in those who have reached venerability is that they realize they cannot rearrange the world according to their heart's desire. Having been through the instructive experience of sin and sadness, they set the trivialities of time against the vast stretches of eternity.

When it comes to troubles, wisdom faces those that

can be solved and shuns the unsolvable. This sounds so simple but many people do not realize that by confronting the unsolvable they deplete themselves and risk bitterness. Those who realize that they lack the time and the energy to heal all the hurts of the world are graced with homeostasis, an aspect of balance, which means they come to terms with self, making the best of things, achieving what is possible, and learning to live with limitations.

There is always the opposite problem of imagining limitations that are not really there. Senescence, for instance, often gets blamed for more than it deserves. If at twenty, for example, you misplaced your keys or failed to remember someone's name, you realized that it was a part of fallibility and did not blame the flaw on the passing of years. After age sixty, though, you are apt to blame every weakness on the accumulated years, as though in youth you had attained perfection.

The wise are aware of ambiguity, the contrary winds blowing across the soul, and observe how good and evil get entangled in the same event. This annoys the foolish because they think everything deserves a yes or a no answer. They don't realize that if you take an interest in the oddness of things, life has more flavor.

The wise notice such strangeness as the way failure can lead to a new strength and success may be a step toward misfortune. A British general put his finger on a truth when he said, "Nothing except a battle lost can be half so melancholy as a battle won," echoing Thomas á Kempis' observation that "the glory of the world is always accompanied by sadness."

Such understanding comes from a certain humility. Humility and humanity are from the Latin root, *humus*, earth. Humility means facing up to your humanity, in other words, getting down to earth.

Those who are down to earth know that God breaks into life in new and startling ways. While grace may arrive in good time, they do not expect it on demand. They do not demand too much certainty, and take for granted that mystery shrouds most important matters.

Long ago a nun gave me a wall-hanging which says: "This is the seedtime not the harvest." She knew how much patience it takes waiting for the harvest.

When students were acting immaturely in the late 1960s, the president of a small western college practically apologized for the tranquility on his campus. "I have a peculiar problem," he said. "Most of our students, and teachers, too, come from the farm. They are used to planting seed and waiting for it to grow, and then harvesting it. They believe in time and in nature. It is hard to get them to take things into their own hands." Surely he must have noticed that most of the problems of the world are caused by impatient, aggressive people who take things into their own hands.

The wise are aware of the long, long stretch between seedtime and harvest.

The aging actress, Elaine Stritch, was walking down a hotel corridor, dressed in her most dazzling foreign creation, when she met a Negro maid.

"You sure got it right on the outside!" said the maid.

"I've got it right on the inside, too," answered the actress.

"Yeah, but I bet it took longer," said the maid.

The wise men and women I have known have not been given to self-pity; so they did not add to the world's collection of infinite distress. They were not members of the cult of self-pity who phone-in during the radio talk shows, or thrust their clenched fists against the sky, or push badly painted signs toward the camera during the evening news. In this Age of Grievance, self-pity stretched out to book length can become a best-seller.

Wise men are so free of self-pity that you get the idea that they would not want you to mourn for them after they are dead. Their attitude in life is reflected in Christina Rosetti's poem: "When I am dead, my dearest, sing no sad songs for me."

The greatest satisfaction in life comes from being used for a high purpose. Those I have admired all seem to have enjoyed that satisfaction. Such sense of high purpose, according to the ancient Greeks, brings *eudaimonia,* happiness. There is happiness in sensing that you are a part of the scheme of things. When living with such awareness there is no telling what interesting events you may stray into.

Your quota of happiness awaits you if you can find satisfaction in a lean life, even prefer it. The Italians have an expression, *l'arte di arrangiarsi,* the art of making do, a wonderful talent.

Old age has a particular happiness reserved for it. It is a different color from the happiness of youth, more muted by far. Consider the mood captured by George Gissing in *The Private Papers of Henry Ryecroft:*

One of the shining moments of my day is that when, having returned a little weary from an afternoon walk, I exchange boots for slippers, out-of-doors coat for easy, familiar, shabby jacket, and, in my deep, soft-elbowed chair, await the tea tray.

Perhaps it is while drinking tea that I most of all enjoy the sense of leisure. In days gone by, I could but gulp down the refreshment, hurried, often harassed, by the thought of the work before me; often I was quite insensible of the aroma, the flavour, of what I drank.

Now, how delicious is the soft yet penetrating odour which floats into my study with the appearance of the teapot! What solace in the first cup, what deliberate sipping of that which follows! What a glow does it bring after a walk in the chilly rain.

Taciturn, embittered rumination is sometimes mistaken for wisdom. A sour stomach has earned some people points they did not deserve. The wise ones I have known have had dispositions somewhat more cheerful than the average. Some even knew joy.

Joy is a rung or two above happiness. It is a grace not detachable such as "We enjoyed the party" or "I enjoyed the opera," but is a current running so deep through the spirit that it even survives suffering. Not even sorrow excludes joy. Real joy does not depend on *having* but is a habit of the soul, a feeling of deep trust in God. The feeling that "God was quite right about that."

As surely as there is a weather of the earth there is a weather of the soul. When the soul's atmosphere is sufficiently benign the joy is there. Leon Bloy felt that joy is the surest sign of the presence of God.

Wisdom does not confuse comfort with civilization. It is possible to have comfort and greatly lack cultivation. The wise also know that luxury is not really an accumulation of things; it is a spiritual matter, a deep satisfaction.

What has been called "the bourgeoisie mentality" lacks the grace of wisdom. The bourgeois man, according to Rene Clare, does not exist without his possessions; he depends for his status on the things he owns, and by himself is not very interesting.

Civility is also a characteristic of the wise. A seventy-seven year old retired engineer in England said: "When you get old you need to have the support of decent manners, you do really."

He might have added that all of society needs the support of decent manners. Civility is the virtue that makes us bearable to one another. While civility keeps a respectful distance between people, insuring privacy, it is also such an endearing characteristic that it attracts, and when it does attract it unites with dignity, not with sentimentality. Courses in civility are more needed than the courses in assertiveness now being offered.

I knew a priest who considered manners "a minor morality." He saw civility as an aspect of *agape, caritas*— charity in the classical meaning of the word.

Politeness not only lessens friction, it is some defense against vulgarity, which Ruskin called "a dead callousness of body and soul." If Ruskin returned to the earth to see the clutter of highways, hear the cacophony of radio, and witness the trivialities of television, he would not expect the paths to be crowded in the pursuit of wisdom.

Fifty years ago Professor Pedro de Landero, a coach at Notre Dame, taught us something about fencing that wise men apply to daily living. He said never watch the opponent's foil too closely. Don't become fascinated or fastened by it. If you do, you lose the ability to shift and parry.

The wise ones do not become too fixed on any one of life's threats. This allows a certain freedom and helps avoid fanaticism. They see through zealotry because they are poignantly aware of what Saint Cyprian called "the sentence passed on the world." He wrote: "This is God's law: That all that has risen shall fall and that all that has grown should wax old, and that strong things should become weak and great things should become small, and that when they have been weakened and diminished they should come to an end."

Those I considered wise had no trouble accepting authority. They felt no need to rebel against the laws of God or man or nature.

Jewish girls singing praises of the ten commandments in Racine's tragedy, *Athalie*, have as their refrain, "O charmante loi." It sounds silly, "O charming law," unless you realize the wisdom of it; accepting and obeying laws spares us anguish beyond enduring.

The wise notice that rebelling against nature is ill advised. One may defy parents, police, Pope and president and get by with it, but nature carries an unseen pair of scales that weighs every defiance, and for every defiance there is a price to pay sooner or later. Momentarily, nature may seem to forgive, but she never forgets where she buried the hatchet.

When all is said and done, the winter of life is not a highly praised season. An Irishman in County Kerry, feeling the burden of his years, said that it would not take much arithmetic to count his blessings, and added, "The trouble with old age is that it hasn't much of a future."

Still winter's season does have the possibility of wisdom. Anyone who wishes to enjoy it in the autumn and even later should plant in the spring. Fortunately, just seeking wisdom is in itself a wise thing.

It was discouraging to hear a specialist in geriatrics say, "A young fool will never be a wise old man." And the rabbis in the Talmud believe that "The wise grow wiser with the years, but the older the ignorant get the more foolish they become."

Here again there is an ambiguity that blows across the human spirit. While old age usually does not change people so much as it unmasks them, it is also true that character can be shaped or shattered by the press of time. A modern rabbi was not speaking only to the young when he said, "You are not only a creature created by divine force, you also possess a divine force within you that can help in the creation of yourself."

An eighty-two year old woman in Wales was so pleased with the changes in herself that she said: "You know new things when you are old and say to yourself, 'I wish I had this much brains when I was young.' Wisdom, you know."

14

The Enemy Within

In a universe where everything is changing, the ways of human nature hold much the same. When you are of an age when your birthday cake can no longer contain all the candles, you become aware of the sameness in humanity. You observe, for instance, that people are often their own worst enemies. The sadness of this flaw I found reflected lately in observations written three hundred years ago by a nun, a piece written early this century in America, and some realizations expressed forty years ago by three prisoners in the Second World War.

In the seventeenth century, a nun wrote a prayer that every old person seeking escape from an unpleasant inner-self, might recite daily:

Lord, thou knowest better than I know myself that I am growing older and will soon be old. Keep me from the fatal habit of thinking I must say something on every subject and on every occasion. Release me from craving to straighten out everybody's affairs. Make me thoughtful but not moody; helpful but not bossy. With my vast store of wisdom it seems a pity not to use it all, but thou knowest, Lord, that I want a few friends at the end.

Keep my mind free from the recital of endless

148

details; give me wings to get to the point. Seal my lips on all my aches and pains. They are increasing and love of rehearsing them is becoming sweeter as the years go by. I dare not ask for grace enough to enjoy the tales of others' pains, but help me to endure them with patience.

I dare not ask for improved memory, but for a growing humility and a lessening cocksureness when my memory seems to clash with the memories of others. Teach me the glorious lesson that occasionally I may be mistaken.

Keep me reasonably sweet; I do not want to be a Saint—some of them are so hard to live with—but a sour old person is one of the crowning works of the devil. Give me the ability to see good things in unexpected places, and talents in unexpected people. And give me, O Lord, the grace to tell them so. Amen.

The nun's prayer is similar to some admonitions written in this century. These reflections about the inner life apply to every age group:

Go placidly amid the noise and haste and remember what peace there may be in silence. As far as possible, without surrender, be on good terms with all persons. Speak your truth quietly and clearly, and listen to others, even the dull and ignorant; they too have their story.

Avoid loud and aggressive persons; they are vexatious to the spirit. If you compare yourself with others, you may become vain and bitter, for always there will be greater and lesser persons than yourself. Enjoy your achievements as well as your plans.

Keep interested in your own career however humble; it is a real possession in the changing fortunes of time. Exercise caution in your business affairs, for the world is full of trickery. But let this not blind you to what virtue there is. Many persons strive for high ideals and life is full of heroism.

Be yourself. Especially do not feign affection. Neither be cynical about love, for in the face of all aridity and disenchantment it is perennial as the grass.

Take kindly the counsel of the years, gracefully surrendering the things of youth. Nurture strength of spirit to shield you in sudden misfortune. But do not distress yourself with imagings. Many fears are born of fatigue and loneliness. Beyond a wholesome discipline, be gentle with yourself.

You are a child of the universe, no less than the trees and the stars. You have a right to be here. And whether or not it is clear to you, no doubt the universe is unfolding as it should.

Therefore be at peace with God, whatever you conceive God to be, and whatever your labors and aspirations. In the noisy confusion of life keep peace with your soul.

With all its sham, drudgery and broken dreams, it is still a beautiful world. Be careful. Strive to be happy.

◊   ◊   ◊

The nun's prayer and the anonymous admonitions are as apt today as they were in the seventeenth century, and they would also have made sense in the Middle Ages and in the Athens of Pericles. Certain themes get played over and over. I am especially aware of that today, having recently read *The Real Enemy* by Pierre d'Harcourt, *Spandau* by Albert Speer, and *The Doctor of the Soul* by Viktor Frankl. The authors experienced such places as Auschwitz, Buchenwald, Dachau, and Spandau. Their observations about the way human beings act are much the same. They all learned, for instance, that hardships make you realize how wonderful an ordinary day really is.

After two years in solitary confinement, Pierre d'Harcourt, formerly of the French Underground, was taken from one prison to another. In his diary he wrote: "As we crossed Paris packed into the back of a van, it was heartrending to have those tantalizing glimpses of the old familiar world, to be so near and yet so far. I remember, too, seeing a few discontented, surly faces and wondered how men and women who had their liberty could look anything but gay and happy."

When being moved from one prison to another, Albert Speer, formerly of the German high command, made a similar observation: "After my long imprisonment this flight in glorious weather was a stirring experience. A moving train, a tugboat on the Elbe, a smoking factory chimney gave me little thrills."

On another occasion Speer wrote in his diary: "As in Nuremberg, the glass of the window has been replaced by cloudy, brownish celluloid. But when I stand on my plain wooden stool and open the transom of the window,

I see the top of an old acacia through the stout iron bars, and at night the stars."

Some imprisoned men find that even terrible things present possibilities for growth. Pierre d'Harcourt said: "In its way solitude is an enriching experience, and it was well that I was able to find it so, for I was to be in solitary confinement for two and a half years. . . . The solitude of prison is an excellent climate for establishing one's interior balance sheet and for internal dialogue which is a necessary function of spiritual life."

Of all the high-ranking Germans imprisoned after the Nuremberg trial, Albert Speer seemed to keep his spiritual balance better than the rest. When Grand Admiral Eric Raeder made this observation, Speer tried to explain his attitude to his diary:

> My temperament may have something to do with it. But it may also come from my ability to organize my life on all planes; the moral aspect of accepting my guilt; the psychic aspect by rejecting almost all deceptive hopes of early release; the practical aspect of disciplining the routine of everyday life, that is, by planning even trivialities: from the cleaning of the cell to dividing time into spells of work and of holiday. Writing down these thoughts is also part of it.

Prisoners learn that extreme hardship makes beasts of some and saints of others. And there is no way of predicting in advance who will fall into which category.

Father Maximilian Kolbe is an example of someone who found sainthood in prison. The Germans, after invading Poland, arrested him because he had harbored Jews. At Auschwitz he shared his meager rations with others and spent time comforting them; many survivors say that he inspired them to go on living.

After an inmate had escaped, in July of 1941, the commandant of Auschwitz arbitrarily selected ten men to be starved to death. When one of them, a Polish Jew, cried out for his wife and children, Kolbe offered to take the man's place.

With prayers, Father Kolbe continued consoling prisoners in the two weeks he survived without food or water. A prison guard finally killed him by injection.

Pope John Paul II presided over Maximilian Kolbe's canonization in October of 1982. The man whose life had been saved told the Pope: "I was never able to thank him, but we looked into each other's eyes before he was hauled away."

Pierre d'Harcourt wrote: "Under the stresses and strains imposed by life in the camp, only one thing prevailed—strength of character. Cleverness, creativeness, learning, all went down; only real goodness survived. . . . Self-discipline was essential, and it is the basis of character."

Dr. Frankl suffered through Auschwitz and Dachau and came out believing that whatever happened to a man's spirit in camp was his own responsibility. As a professor of psychiatry and neurology at the University of Vienna it was inevitable that he live those dark days as a professional observer.

You are spiritually responsible for what hardship "makes" of you, he decided. Your inner freedom remains for you to give some shape to your existence. You retain the possibility of deciding for or against the influence of your surroundings.

Dr. Frankl wrote in *Doctor of the Soul:* "There are plenty of examples—often heroic ones—to prove that even in these camps men could still 'do differently'; that they did not have to submit to the apparently almighty concentration-camp laws of psychic deformation. . . . Probably in every concentration-camp there were individuals able to overcome their apathy and suppress irritability. There were the ones who were examples of renunciation and self-sacrifice. Asking nothing for themselves, they went about on the grounds and in the barracks of the camp, offering a kind word here, a crust of bread there."

He would agree with the last paragraph of Pierre d'Harcourt's *The Real Enemy:* "The camp showed me that a man's real enemies are not ranged against him along the border of a hostile country; they are often among his own people, indeed, within his own mind. The worst enemies are hate, and greed, and cruelty. The real enemy is within."

The nun and the anonymous writer who lived in Baltimore long ago would agree with the observations the three prisoners made. They would all agree that bitter souls abandon themselves to destruction when they ought to be building something inside themselves.

The elderly might learn something from all of this. They need to accept the problems of advanced age as part of their final vocation. Those who took such an attitude toward the horrors of the prison fared better than the rest. The saints became their own best selves.

An unfortunate thing about bitter people is that they never become the remarkable individuals that they are capable of becoming. According to an Hasidic tale, before his death, Rabbi Zusya said: "In the coming world, they will not ask me: 'Why were you not Moses?' They will ask me: 'Why were you not Zusya?'"

15

Go Gentle into
that Good Night

An elderly gentleman in Dublin observed: "Nobody gets out of this life alive!"

An Irish blacksmith advised me: "Live every day as though it is your last, and one day you'll be right."

A judge in County Wicklow said: "We have been born into a world where three out of every three people die."

The Irish more readily speak of death than do Americans. In this country two subjects of conversation remain taboo: God and death. You may announce that a relative or friend has died, but don't speak of death as inevitable. Most people prefer to feel exempt. Their attitude is that "the captains and the kings depart" but not me!

The subject of death displeases even those who believe in a brighter prospect. Monsignor Ronald Knox, when told that he would soon die, said, "One clings, and I can't think why. You would have thought anyone would prefer heaven to fruit juice."

One clings because the instinct to survive goes to the depths of being, and so the human race endures. The instinct need not be invoked; it is there all the time—when a car bears down on you, you jump aside without any act of will.

If the instinct to survive is so natural, it might seem that to accept death would be unnatural. Yet dying is the most natural thing in the world. It is the great leveler, and everybody is equal in its democracy. As the lament from Shakespeare's *Cymbeline* has it:

> Golden lads and girls all must
> As chimney-sweepers come to dust.

Freud did not believe in immortality. People promote such notions, he said, because deep down inside they deny death.

Jung felt there must be some sort of immortality because all of the mythologies in the world contain a belief in it. Surely, he said, all of those people were not wrong through the centuries.

Kierkegaard thought that "immortality is no learned question." It is something to be sensed by looking into one's soul.

What happens after death is not something to argue about now. You realize this when standing in awe of creation. Astronomers, for instance, say that there are billions of stars in our galaxy, and that billions of galaxies inhabit the universe, and that there may well be billions of universes. With this awesome awareness you are willing to say that whatever happens after death is part of the Creator's plan, and that is good enough for you. You won't feel that it is fitting to try to second guess, or give directions.

Learning to accept the fact of death takes time. First, you learn to accept the deaths of those you care about. The older you get the more your past resembles a church-yard with a winding path lined with stones, all memorials to good memories.

At a funeral, after a certain age, you mourn two deaths—that of your friend and that of some part of your past. All of those blank spaces and silences become over-whelming. No one is left to share your in-jokes or mem-ories. No one remembers you when you were in your prime. You become a stranger in the world. An elderly English lady said with some wistfulness: "Now that Sarah Watts is gone, no one on Pomeroy Hill will ever again call me Nellie."

In time the inner landscape of yourself, once well-forested, has only a few sparse trees here and there. When most of his friends were dead, a distraught Jona-than Swift wrote to Alexander Pope: "You are the only one left to me now—be so kind as to outlive me."

When friends and relatives die you need to take the emotion long invested in them and shift it to something else. Such flexibility may make the difference between a tranquil and a mournful old age.

In the presence of death, especially your own, you realize how brief life is. There is no such thing as a long life. Anyone who says, even facetiously, "I am not long for this world," speaks the truth. Saint Teresa of Avila said, "We are all going to die in a couple of hours."

Life's brevity has always haunted old age. As Job put it, "The days fly swifter than a weaver's shuttle."

An Indian chief, well into his eighties, observed that

even a long life is like "the breath of the buffalo in the wintertime."

A Buddhist monk, at ninety, thought that "life is more transient than the dew."

An English priest, on his seventy-fifth birthday, said, "I think about how little time I have left—ten years, five years. And looking back ten years I think 'yesterday!' Just yesterday. So looking forward to even ten years is only looking forward to tomorrow. Tomorrow it will end."

Time flies faster each year. The ear hears the ticking clock less well, but the heart hears it louder and louder. Schopenhauer likened the passing of time to a ball that starts slowly and picks up speed as it rolls downhill. Or to change the image, time is like a rotating disc—the greater distance you move from the center, the start of life, the more swiftly you travel.

When such awareness of time's swiftness sweeps over you, it might well make life more precious. Orientals feel that transience is part of the loveliness of the universe. Living flowers are more cherished than artificial ones because of the poignancy of their passing.

How should you act when face-to-face with someone who is about to depart this life? You may find the word death hard to say because it has such a solemn sound, like the deepest bell in a carillon. The tendency then is to chat of trivialities, and with forced gaiety ease the uneasiness. Projects that the dying person will never carry out are spoken of as though they will be: the garden to be planted, the book to be written, the trip to be enjoyed.

It is easy to speak of earthly trips, but difficult to talk

of the ultimate journey. Whether or not you should talk about it, I think, depends on how the dying person feels in this matter. We are so different. Some people need to be surrounded by relatives and friends in the final days, and others, embarrassed by attention, prefer benign neglect, wanting to go it alone. When visiting the dying, what you prefer is not important; it is the dying person's preference that counts. Only sensitivity will tell you what that is.

Widows in primitive societies used to commit suicide. Even today some widows kill their own spirits with excessive mourning. Some widowers do, too, but since women outlive men by eight years there are not so many widowers around. A French psychiatrist observed that those who had the best marriages tend to bear separation best. "The most unconsolable sorrows," he said, "are those that are kept alive by a guilty conscience."

Getting ready to live without friends or relatives means never using anybody as a crutch. Husbands and wives need to give a shape to their individual lives so as to carry on in an admirable way beyond the other's death.

Inner resources are what help avoid inner collapse. Things that absorb attention, and seem worth doing, and bring satisfaction help develop a new life with quiet dignity.

The *Bhagavad Gita* admonishes: "Over the inevitable thou shouldst not grieve." Epictetus, born a slave shortly after Christ died, spoke of how to prepare yourself for inevitabilities. When you have affection for something, he said, make yourself doubly conscious of its nature. "Then when your favorite jug breaks, or your best friend dies, you will be prepared; your awareness of their natures makes you realize they could not be around for ever."

As funerals of friends arrive at shorter intervals, life becomes more and more a time of faint handshakes and mumbled sympathies. Each casket serves as an admonition, a kind of sermon. You will best accept this, while waiting to join the great majority, if you have fulfilled your vocation. Then there will be a sense of rounding off, of final curtain: here is a good place to get off. You will feel sympathy with a saying common in the Sahara: "Drink from the well and yield your place to another."

Dylan Thomas exhorted his father:

Do not go gentle into that good night
Old age should burn and rave at close of day
Rage, rage against the dying of the light

Strange advice from a poet. Poets are supposed to love truth, and mortality is the most definite truth around. As a poet he should have been sensitive to pattern. Anyone who sees death as completion of a pattern, said Spinoza, is apt to accept it with some grace. So to rage is immature and out of touch with reality. Besides it won't do any good.

If you meet death with a certain courtesy it is easier on doctors, nurses, friends, and relatives. So for the sake of others it is best to die with dignity.

A good way to approach the end is described by Ivan Turgenev in *Diary of a Superfluous Man:* "The last of the earthy vanities disappears in the face of death. I feel a calm coming over me. Everything is becoming so simple, so clear."

Hundreds of people who have been declared dead and then revived speak of the simplicity and clarity. They were all aware of a great light and a warm sense of peace and agree that now they no longer fear the dying day.

The most admirable attitude toward death is expressed in four words of the Lord's Prayer: "Thy will be done." Such acceptance is included in the way Epictetus saw things. He was aware that death is a part of the great script, a working out of a divine plan:

> Remember you are acting in a play, and the Playwright chooses the manner of it. If he wants it short it is short; if long, it is long. If he wants you to act a poor man you must act the part with all your powers, and the same if your part be that of a cripple, or a magistrate, or a plain man. For your business is to act the character that is given you and act it well. The choice of the cast is Another's.

It is well to realize that your manner in leaving the stage is part of your performance. It does not greatly change the world, though. Life goes on: a bluejay chases a robin, a girl dials a telephone, and an old man lights his pipe. The day you die is just another day.

If you are graced with the attitude of an Epictetus, you attain what the ancients called "the height of philosophy by dying well." It can then be said of you what Shakespeare said of the Thane of Cawdor: "Nothing in his life became him like his leaving it."

16

Pursuing Peace of Mind

Joshua Loth Liebman said that when he was a brash youth he compiled an inventory of earthly desirables: health, love, beauty, talent, fame, fortune. When he showed the list to a rabbi the old man said, "You have missed the most important ingredient. Without it every possession becomes a torment."

"What's that?" asked Liebman.

The rabbi took a pencil and wrote: "Peace of mind." He went on to say that this is a gift God reserves for his special protégés. "Talent and beauty he gives to many," said the rabbi. "Wealth is commonplace. Fame is not rare. But peace of mind he bestows charily. Most are never blessed with it. Many wait out their lives, far into old age, wishing for the gift to descend on them."

The rabbi is right in feeling that without peace of mind everything seems shallow, but from the way he put it I sense that he sees peace of mind as something given away free in a sort of celestial lottery. He makes it sound as though you wait, and if you are lucky it comes sailing in out of the blue. The individual, I think, needs to make some effort in the pursuit of serenity and has some say as to whether or not it arrives.

In Japan I met Father Gerald Griffin who tries to help people find peace of mind before he begins talking to them about theology. Religion does best in a healthy psyche, he decided during his studies in counseling at Sophia, the Jesuit university in Tokyo, and at Saint Paul's University in Ottawa, Canada.

"We have to relate to the whole person," said Father Griffin. "We have to be aware of his feelings, hopes, fears, and his desire for acceptance by others. And our teaching must be experienced. A Chinese proverb seems apt: 'I heard and I forget; I see and I remembered; I do and I understand.'

"That Chinese proverb might well be a Japanese proverb, for these are pragmatic people. They value an idea depending on how it can be tested in this life. They feel that missionaries tend to overemphasize the spiritual and eternal, making secular life unimportant. The Japanese cannot believe that this world is unimportant."

During his university studies Father Griffin decided that the findings of psychology and of group dynamics are something a missionary might use. So he developed a course to help people come to a degree of self-knowledge and self-acceptance, feeling that they might then be better able to receive the messages of any religion.

Father Griffin finds that many people approach religious instruction full of self-rejection. Behind self-hatred he finds an excess of pride; humility is needed for self-acceptance. He has learned that accepting self is not something done once-and-for-all, but is a continuous unfolding. It is possible to accept yourself in midlife but not in old age, in health but not in sickness, in good times but not in bad.

Before he starts talking about religion, Father Griffin spends many weeks leading small groups in discussion. They talk about such things as the art of listening, self-hatred, and maturity. These help people explore their feelings, to look at their self-images and see themselves in a better light.

"At first most participants are shy and reluctant to talk," said Father Griffin, "but as the brave ones start the ball rolling, the members gradually develop a feeling of trust in one another. Others begin to speak up and tell things about themselves that they had never been able to tell anyone before. They say that they experience a feeling of great relief after unburdening themselves. Listening to shared problems makes them realize that they are not alone. This is comforting."

Changes brought about in the lives of some of the participants have been remarkable—changes that surprise themselves, their families, teachers, and friends. An outstanding example, Mrs. Yamashita, seventy-seven, started the course depressed and down on life. She woke up each morning hoping it would be her last so that she could join her daughter who had died. Her two married daughters dreaded visiting her; she seemed to have no time for them and was fussy and demanding.

Mrs. Yamashita found the course unpleasant at first and after each session promised herself that she would not come again. But she did. In the beginning she was a pest. She would say that her eyes were bad and that she couldn't see the blackboard, but as time went on she mellowed, and even her eyesight seemed to improve. She changed so much that people liked associating with her. She became the group matriarch. Her teacher, Miss

Yoshida, said, "You have changed from a crabapple to an apricot."

Mrs. Yamashita said that her family likes to visit her again, now that she has found new meaning in life. Instead of thinking about how much she would like to die, she wonders what she might do to help other people. She has become a counselor for other old people who come to her with troubles. She used to disdain the meetings of the elderly, but now attends them, and her very presence brightens the day. She is now ready to accept religion and not do damage to it. She is a more holy person.

Father Griffin sees old age as a time of unmasking. Bones and veins show more readily and the deeper self is exposed as never before. If there is to be peace of mind, religion is especially needed then. One needs to believe that one's final destiny is more important than that of an autumn leaf. Without an anchor in religion one is apt to hurtle through life lacking stability of soul. Everybody needs to worship something; if not God, then it will be some sorry substitute—an addiction, or money, or power.

In old age the body cells no longer renew themselves with alacrity, but the spirit can still be vigorous. The body's decline is not tragic but the disinclination of the soul is, especially if some power remains but the desire to act is gone. Not to lose elasticity of spirit, after muscles stiffen, takes some striving. Sainte-Beuve said, "There are people whose watch stops at a certain hour and who remain permanently at that age."

Your choice is either rebirth or ossification, as Mrs. Yamashita learned. You need to keep upgrading the product, a matter of becoming more fulfilled at each phase of life. You need to try to surpass yourself—not others, only yourself.

Through inner growth even an old man in a wheel-chair can grow. When Teilhard de Chardin was ill a friend said, "His spirit seemed to draw strength from the weakness of his body." Even when bedridden the problem is to keep some inner control. There are still options: you can become bitter, feel sorry for yourself, and turn into a pest, or you can show an attitude so admirable as to give courage to all who come near you. When you can no longer overcome limitations by actions you may still do so by attitude.

Inner growth is not a matter of rearranging the furniture of the soul. For instance, books of check-lists that tell you how to better arrange your time are stop-gap measures. Only when the spirit flourishes from healthy values does life fall naturally into place, and no artificial check-list is needed.

Dorothy Sayers said that the difference between the mind of a maker and the Mind of the Maker is "a difference, not of category, but only of quality and degree." If you want, as the old spiritual directors used to say, to do God's will, that very attitude organizes your interests, emotions and destiny; you have found a synthesis to give unity to impulses, actions, and experiences. And since the grace of a pure contemplative is rare, most of us need a more mundane vocation to serve as a bridge to the Almighty.

In old age we begin to see what life is all about, said Father John La Farge, S.J. "We see what the Creator has made of us, and what he is trying to fashion in our minds and hearts." In the closing years we are apt to find God's work in small, unspectacular events. To discover God in our own experience of life is spiritual growth.

Mrs. Yamashita found peace of mind because she worked at replacing poor attitudes with rich ones. Dom Hubert Van Zeller wrote: "If a weak person does a strong thing, he is more likely to do another strong thing than if he had stuck in the practice of doing weak ones. However weak a person is, or however strong a person is, the repetition of the act, for good or for evil, transforms the person's character."

Buddhist monks have also taught for centuries that we are the heirs of our actions. We seem to know that intuitively, for if we come across someone unhappy with his lot, we are often tempted to shake him and say, "If you want to inherit a better self, live life in a better way!" You are the one who determines minute by minute what you will become. Where you are at this moment is not so important as where you are going. And if in the present you desert ideals and lower standards, that will age you more than wrinkles.

The tendency is to slight the present by constant anticipation. Yet by the time you are old you should have noticed that when the future becomes the present it too will have about it a gray dailiness. The transcending moments are rare. Usually they cannot be foreseen or prepared for. Yet the present has the possibilities of grace, if only you lay yourself open to it.

You will never dispose of confusion in your life in one fell swoop. To expect to do so is like expecting a badly conditioned body to become fit within a day or to lose pounds of unwanted weight overnight. If you are backed into a corner mentally, physically, or spiritually, it took time to get yourself there and it will take time to get out. The modern temperament, demanding instant results, is impatient with slow unfolding, which is nature's way. It is hard to admit that a life lived askew for three-score years cannot be put into immediate alignment.

In exploring life you must willingly redraw your maps from time to time. No matter what area you explore—especially in spiritual terrain—you never have it fully scouted. In exploring you won't advance in a straightforward march. If you are fortunate, the rhythm is two steps forward and one back. Sometimes it is one forward and ten back, followed by a rush of a dozen forward. This can be disheartening, and yet any forward movement is a stay against decline.

Spirits in decline reflect immaturity and lack symmetry. Balance is a characteristic of maturity. The immature tend toward extremes. The balance, for instance, between cowardness and rashness is courage, between unsureness and impulsiveness is control, between stinginess and extravagance is generosity.

A deadly imbalance is the show of concern for outer needs more than for inner ones. Survivors of Europe's prison camps, as quoted earlier, agree that those who cared only for the body died; those who did something to keep alive the inner life had a better chance for survival.

No one will have peace of mind without balance. You will go off balance if you let either prosperity or misfortune cause too much of a whirlpool at the core. It was for good reason that at the temple at Delphi was carved: Nothing to excess.

An awareness of God's presence in the world is more important in old age than in youth. Without such we tend to die even before our official deaths. As Dag Hammarskjold wrote in his diary: "God does not die on the day when we cease to believe in a personal deity, but we die on the day when our lives cease to be illuminated by the steady radiance, renewed daily, of a wonder, the source of which is beyond all reason."

No one can describe God without setting limits. We are stuck within the limitations of the comprehensible, and to act as though we can get beyond leads to bad religion. Saint Augustine said, "Thou canst understand naught about God, for he is above all understanding."

Mother Marguerite, a Carmelite nun in the seventeenth century, said, "The spiritual life is constituted in very few words and a very great inclination to God."

A simple man, Brother Laurence, living in a Paris monastery of Carmelites in the seventeenth century, showed an attitude worth imitating. Prayers in the ordinary sense ceased, in time, to have meaning for him. "I have quitted all forms of devotion and all set prayers except those to which my position of a friar obliges me." He offered as a continuous prayer his vocation: "With me, my time of labor is no longer different from that of prayer. In his service I turn the cake that is on the pan before me." Approaching his work in the kitchen he said: "Be with me in this my endeavor, accept the labor of my hands, fill my heart as always." Having completed the task he would ask himself how he had performed; if well, he gave thanks, and if badly he asked forgiveness. Brother Laurence said we delude ourselves if we consider the time of prayer as different from other times. The only way to pray twenty-four hours a day is by wanting to do the will of God.

Brother Laurence's approach to the Almighty is in contrast to that of many people. A recent survey shows that ninety-five percent of those interviewed believe in God, but only fifty-four percent feel that such belief has any influence on their life's work.

Years ago on a farm in County Cork an Irish family and its servants gathered each evening at nine for prayers. One of the farm boys was usually late. The head of the house said, "It's for only ten minutes, Kevin, ten minutes to give Almighty God."

"Yes, sir," replied Kevin—"they are the longest ten minutes of the day."

But this does not necessarily mean that Kevin was failing as a man of prayer. Words formulated by someone else and recited in a crowded parlor may not have been his way. Who knows how much he worshiped while walking through the fields that God created? Maybe Kevin's way was explained by Saint Paul when he said that the invisible must be understood through the visible.

Charles Kingsley wrote: "When I walk in the fields I am oppressed now and then with an innate feeling that everything I see has a meaning, if I could but understand it. And this feeling of being surrounded with truths which I cannot grasp amounts to an indescribable awe sometimes."

Between my sixtieth and seventieth birthdays I explored many religions while writing books set in Korea, Burma, Fiji, China, Japan and the Philippines. I came to respect any belief that reveres something beyond the human self, and came to realize what Saint John of the Cross meant when he said that no two men go more than halfway on the same road to God.

Although a member of a specific sect, it is well to be aware of the universal expression of religious belief. The Vedas declare: "As the different streams having their sources in different places all mingle their waters in the Great Sea, O Lord, similarly the different faiths which men follow, through different tendencies and temperaments, various though they appear, crooked or straight, all lead to thee."

Aware of different tendencies and temperaments, Origen, a Christian theologian in the third century, advocated two types of religion: an esoteric one fully aware of mystery for the highly educated, and a religion of myths and legends for the uneducated. He felt that for peace of mind one's religion must "fit."

One learns about religion as a child and so there is always the possibility that it will remain at a childish level. Some people do not seem to mind, especially if they have remained immature in other ways. If, however, old age brings an unfolding maturity, religion, too, should be explored at some depth. The explorers will find a variety of needs; some will prefer the rigidity of dogma and others the subtlety of mystery.

As for worship, no committee can design a mode of worship that is right for everyone. The manner of worship that comes most naturally is determined by the kind of person you are. In your preference you reveal your inner self; you give yourself away. For example, the contemplative and the activist are not apt to feel at ease in the same manner of worship. Those who prefer the East's silence and serenity will find in the ways of the West too much fidgeting and activity.

The great essential, though, is an awareness of God's presence in the world, one that should increase with age. Just as when you hear a sound and are aware it comes from a piano—that sound and a piano are united in your consciousness—so if all aspects of creation make you aware of the Creator, that is worship.

There should also be the awareness that the God we approach is picayune compared with the real God beyond our comprehension. We are stuck with speaking of the true God in ways that are only dimly true because we just can't do any better. As Blaise Pascal observed: "Reason's last step is the recognition that there are an infinite number of things which are beyond it. It is merely feeble if it does not go as far as to realize that."

A true Christian is one who is a Christian because it is his nature to be so. And so it is with true Jews, and true Moslems, and adherents to other religions. In every religion there are the naturals and the artificials. The artificials become engrossed with all the rules and regulations; they turn religion into a form of bookkeeping—so many this and so many that.

Approaches to the spiritual life are beyond numbering. Balzac, for instance, said that the first hermits "lived with God and inhabited the world which is most populated, the world of the spirits." Hermits searched for the place that made them feel closest to God. While God is the same everywhere, we are not the same everywhere, and so we need to search for the place that is best for us.

Some people, at their best when involved in the lives of others, need group worship because the solitude of inner worship does not become them. Those given to contemplation, however, are able to organize their solitude and may find that all the body chemistry and vibrations of large groups blur inner peace.

Spiritual growth, the best defense against loneliness, is encouraged in highly individual ways. For instance, James Jones, an English curate, said that he kept a journal for the sake of deliverance. After a long interval of failing to make entries, he wrote, in 1786: "I really believe my neglecting to journalize has very much contributed to my soul's decline in spiritual things." Five years later he felt, "The good effects arising from my frequent use of my diary are hardly to be imagined. It leads to reflection and self-conversion which is not one of the least among its good effects."

A Buddhist writer and Saint Augustine agree that you reach holiness and maturity when you can follow what your heart desires without transgressing what is right. It is not a matter of fighting off evil but of preferring good, and stepping beyond asceticism into that realm of spirit where wisdom is found. As Saint Augustine phrased it: "Happy is the man who has everything he desires providing he desires nothing amiss."

A French writer, Charles de Montalembert, said that in old age those who lead the lives of religious might well spread *benegnitas*, a benevolence of high order. He thought this the rightful final stage of their vocation. A benevolence of high order might well be the final stage of everyone's vocation. You emanate something right up to the end, whether or not you want to. If it is not hope, courage and faith, it is apt to be bitterness, despair and cynicism. You brighten or darken the days of others unless you stay well-concealed behind closed doors.

Self-pity probably destroys more benignity in the elderly than anything else. As Martha Graham, at eighty-four said: "Pity is something to be avoided like the plague. I don't feel it for anyone else and I don't feel it for myself."

Benignity is reflected in a poem written by Saint Teresa of Avila and translated by Longfellow:

Let nothing disturb thee;
Nothing affright thee;
All things are passing;
God never changeth;
Patient endurance
Attaineth to all things;
Who God possesseth
In nothing is wanting;
Alone God sufficeth.

When haunted by a gradual dimming of the lights we speak of death, wondering how it will be when our shadows no longer fall upon the earth. It is then, said Jung, that problems are more apt to be spiritual than psychological. Then some sort of faith is necessary for mental health, a theme developed by William Sergant in *The*

British Journal of Psychiatry. That is because human beings persist in searching for something satisfying, yearning to worship something worth worshiping, and wondering, "What does it all mean?" Such hauntings can be allayed only by faith.

Since spiritual problems are best eased by developing a religious view of life, Koreans show oriental wisdom in a custom called *hwankap.* On their sixtieth birthdays, after a grand celebration, the guests of honor are supposed to retire to spend their days seeking serenity and so enlarge their religious concerns.

Serenity and wholeness in a well-formed old age come when you sense that if you lead the life you should, everything will end well. This is a consolation, but not one hundred percent consolation, because part of being human is learning to live with a degree of uncertainty. To have the courage of your doubts, as time runs out, may be more difficult than having the courage of your convictions.

After living long enough you are apt to agree with C.S. Lewis who wrote, at age sixty-four, that there are no non-religious activities, only religious and irreligious. Religion is not a department of life, but a saturation of life. This allows no split between what a person does and a person's professed religion.

The greatest damage the mass media have done is train us to see things in compartments. Through their great stress on such things as politics, funded programs and bureaucracy, they have led us to feel that our fate depends on others and forget that it depends mostly on the health of our individual souls.

The media hawk tragedies without putting them into perspective. Spinoza, who would never have been interviewed on the evening news, believed that tragedies are trivial things when seen in the perspective of eternity. Once you share that belief, troubles no longer diminish you but call out your powers. This insight is a grace that comes from spiritual resources beyond yourself, a comfort that can be the greatest gift of old age. As a grace it can be asked for and worked for but not demanded.

No matter how much your religious view expands with age, it is always narrow, just as every view of the universe, no matter how broad, is embarrassingly restricted. Those who approach religion through theology and philosophy have a different view from those who find their way through broken lives, their own and others'. The mystic's view is vastly different from that of the activist. That our view of religion and of God is narrow is somewhat disturbing, especially in old age. Not to admit it, though, is more silly and arrogant than standing at the edge of the Atlantic saying, "Now, I have seen the ocean in its entirety, every last wave."

By the time you reach old age you might begin to realize that religion is not *knowing* God but being aware of a Presence in the world. Then you may see all of creation as a cathedral where every well-disposed action is an act of worship and understand that it is not the mind that prays but the person: worship is a way of being. Such an insight is also a gift, something to be asked for. Even the apostles said, "Lord, teach us to pray."

Since there is a flaw in everything created, nothing in life is fully satisfying; everything lets you down somewhat. Only the peace of mind that comes with faith keeps life from seeming absurd. Without it all bank accounts, insurance policies, and physical checkups fail to assuage a terrible gnawing.

Some people feel the gnawing so much that the grimace of anxiety is carved into their faces. Anxiety is worse than fear. A fear has a rational basis; it is directed toward something definite—tornadoes, mad dogs, drunk drivers. But anxiety is vague, persistent and haunting. Such haunting leads to despondency or to faith. Arnold Toynbee said "I believe that any challenge when it gets down to the quick, when it puts you really up against it, brings you face-to-face with religion."

Religion makes life add up to something even when you cannot make sense of the world. It is a defense against spiritual aloneness, which is worse than social aloneness.

The diminishments of age can cause uneasiness of spirit in so many ways. For instance, Ronald Blythe noticed one of them while talking with elderly monks in England. He found that they could face death more readily than the decline of spiritual passion. "Prayer is not what it was," said Blythe. "Although the monks try to reignite its flames with every technique known to them, it barely sparks. As one of them said, 'So often having nothing to offer, he offers Nothingness.'"

That monk knows he must make an effort for peace of mind. Such peace is a great richness, a harvest of spiritual growth. That is why the rabbi valued it so much and why Father Griffin worked hard to help Mrs. Yamashita attain it.

17

Beyond the Holy Roman Empire and Hula Hoops

While you are better off than the Mayfly which lives only a day, the difference is really quite slight when your own short span is measured against the unendingness of eternity. That is why President Reagan was being obvious when he predicted that Communism will end in the dustbin of history—everything does, from the Holy Roman Empire to hula hoops.

Until you realize that all of creation suffers the Mayfly flaw, you might live as though you have time ad infinitum—which brings to mind the story about the devil asking his helpers for ideas as to how he might better misinform people.

A green demon said, "Tell them there is no God."

"We do that," said the Old Man.

Another apprentice suggested, "Tell them there is no heaven."

"We do that, too."

An old hand said, "Tell them there is no hurry."

He feared that when you truly realize you suffer the Mayfly flaw, you may become interested in a life of the spirit.

That newfound interest, however, has its dilemmas.

For one thing, you may want to see far in advance. I experienced this, symbolically, one night on Cheju Island, off the southern coast of Korea. Never have I known such darkness as obstructed five miles of my route across alien ground. The dull glow of a borrowed flashlight revealed only the next step, but that was all that was needed. Yet I kept wanting more light to see far ahead.

If the spirit lightens one step, that is enough, for your effectiveness grows in the present. You are fortunate if you cherish the present as Claudel did when he wrote in his journal: "Some sigh for yesterday! Some for tomorrow. But you must reach old age before you can understand the meaning—the splendid, absolute, unchallengeable, irreplaceable meaning—of the word today."

Santayana had that feeling at eighty-two when he wrote to a friend: "And the charm I find in old age—for I was never happier than I am now—comes of having learned to live in the moment, and thereby in eternity: and this means recovering a perpetual youth, since nothing can be fresher than each day as it dawns and changes."

Another problem that comes with a new-found interest in the inner life is trying to rationalize things of the spirit. That is as senseless as trying to derationalize mathematics. The spirit is the province of mystery, of things beyond understanding. If they could be comprehended they would be mere puzzles. Puzzles exist in our realm, but mysteries are of a different realm. Puzzles intrigue and frustrate, but mysteries, sensed and wondered at, enhance the spirit.

If in old age you come to care about the inner life,

inner victories will outnumber outward losses. You will, of course, still find dark depths in the soul, but also splendor. Unless you cater to the splendor, dark things keep bubbling up, among which is the attitude expressed in Lamentations: "See whether there is any sorrow like mine!" Such complaints cast shadows over everything, inside and out.

How useless to complain unless something can come from it! Griping about poor bus service might help, but singing the blues about a rainy day is silly. (It is delightful on a rainy morning in Lisbon to see all of those colorful umbrellas; that is what enlivens drab days—brightness, not dark looks.)

What Henry James called the "imagination of disaster" is highly developed in our time. Perhaps it was always so; certainly some Old Testament prophets sounded as though the end will come by midnight on Friday.

The other extreme is a belief in the nearness of utopia. Even the utopians, out of frustration, sometimes develop the "imagination of disaster." The most symmetrical approach is to follow the Greek admonition, "Nothing to excess." Then you will neither anticipate disaster nor expect paradise on earth. You may then see the glory in the journey and not stall the inner life at one place, but let it travel along a road. In the *Anabasis* almost every chapter ends, "And the next day he was again going forward." With such inner unfolding you should, by old age, have special access to the wonder of the world.

Some dark-spirited people have a propensity for the dour, almost an affection for it. Even when things go their way they are unwilling to feel fortunate. Never do they put off until tomorrow any worrying they can do today. Father Leo R. Ward, at age ninety, wrote of life in a retirement home: "Our problem is ourselves. Most of us are old and decrepit and cranky."

Darkness of spirit is infectious, like influenza. Many a day is ruined by another's disgruntled mood. To steal a day is a serious matter; better to steal a wallet. You can return money, but stolen time is irreplaceable.

John Tracy Ellis named Thomas More and Cardinal Newman as his heroes because each knew how to accept adversity. They did not react to hurts by baring their wounds. Thomas More accepted harsh treatment and death "with extraordinary charity," wrote Father Ellis, and as for Newman, "I was first attracted to him by his literary style, but more important than literary grace was the pathos of his life. Amid all reverses, shabby treatment from superiors, frustrations and slights, Newman was hurt but never bitter."

Such noble men bring to mind a line from Ecclesiasticus: "For these maintain the fabric of the world."

Thomas More and Cardinal Newman had the gift of acceptance, known as sanctity. And they followed their inner promptings, by which I don't mean conscience saying, no, stop, avoid, but urgings saying, yes, do, go!

When speaking of promptings which had set a direction for his life as a missionary, an old priest said, "I had to hasten on, to catch up with my vision." In following his promptings he emanated a serenity, a sense of calm good sense, and seemed under control; his life was not flying off in all directions. He proved that it is possible to have control of the spirit even when his physical condition declined to where he decided to give up his driver's license. (That voluntary decision—not one demanded from the outside—reflects control and good sense.)

By following your promptings you discover what you ought to be doing, and that brings a sense of adequacy, something everybody needs. To get that feeling, you will have to settle for less than perfection, accepting life as a blending of success and failure, of good and bad. If you insist on believing the possibility of perfection, you will create problems for yourself and for others.

By the time you are well into the afternoon of life you should have learned to live with what you perceive as your deficiencies. You are not pretty, you lack coordination, you are shy, and a hundred other things you wish were not so. To let this ruin your life is foolish. Long ago Democritus said: "It is unreasonableness not to submit to the necessary conditions of life. People are fools who live without enjoyment of life." To enjoy a feeling of adequacy you need to find satisfaction in activities not hampered by your deficiencies.

In life there are more roads not taken than taken; to spend time fretting over those not taken is silly. It leads to lowered self-esteem, which is not the same as humility. Low self-esteem comes from selfishness and pride and mars the spirit; humility enriches it because it focuses on God more than on self.

Venerable old people with a sense of significance make things easier for everybody. Much is written about how society should make its old people feel respectable, but that feeling comes from within, and is earned. The verb "earned" cannot be overstressed; the aura of respectability and significance needs a day to day effort. Grace, style, charm and quality can be lost; they are not gifts made in perpetuum.

A lack of spiritual growth brings the feeling of moral failure, one of emptiness. To fill the void the tendency is to pour in things, things, and more things. The more poured in, the emptier life may feel. Lasting satisfaction comes from beyond the graspable.

In our culture where the material rates above the spiritual, the prevailing opinion is that you are to be pitied if you cannot afford everything advertised. Yet if you have been paying attention to the way life works, you may have noticed that not wanting much has a great freedom about it. When your needs and wants are the same, the spirit has a chance to grow. If in retirement you still put high hopes in accumulated things, you have failed to learn much about life while living it.

Clinging to things may have little to do with real need. Clinging can lead to imagined destitution. In her autobiography, *The Journey*, Countess Sternberg tells of meeting an old friend, one of the Rothschilds, and of having the friend go to great lengths bewailing her poverty. Later the countess said to one of the Rothschild relatives, "Surely she can't be as poor as she says she is!" The relative replied, "Of course not. It's all in her mind. It's pitiful, really. She clings to money as if it were life itself. But then I'm afraid it's all she has left to cling to now."

Mother Teresa, a servant of the poor in Calcutta, compared two kinds of poverty: "Maybe in the United

States we don't see the hungry and the naked and the homeless in the streets. But I think there is a much greater poverty. By giving to a person who is hungry for a piece of bread or for a plate of rice, you have already solved the difficulty. But, I think, the people who are hurt, who are lonely, who are unwanted, who are hopeless, who are those like alcoholics and the people who have forgotten how to smile, who have forgotten what are human love and human touch—I think that is a very great poverty."

The nun has observed that materialism leads to a kind of destitution. The spendthrift becomes poor and the miser suffers his own kind of poverty, for as the Chinese say, "He who hoards much loses much."

A spiritual journey is the way to escape such poverty, and accept adversity, and live with your shortcomings and other of life's troubles. A physical journey can be realized—you finally do reach Pretoria—but a spiritual one needs to carry right up to the requiem. Fortunately, when you begin a journey in search of God you have to some extent found him because you cannot look for anything without some concept of it. Such a search, the best of disciplines, is an organizing force that gives unity to life. Without unity life might seem absurd, a horrible drama difficult to take part in or even sit through.

Even if lacking a definite religious orientation it is well to cultivate moral values, at least enough to help you behave yourself. Otherwise false pleasures that bedevil you will spoil all real pleasures. Morality makes sense even when honored for selfish reasons.

Meditation and contemplation have long been considered good for the spirit. In the Middle Ages, Richard of Saint Victor, described the difference between the two spiritual exercises: "Meditation with great mental industry plods along the steep and laborious road keeping the end in view. Contemplation on a free wing circles around with great nimbleness wherever the impulse takes it. Meditation investigates; contemplation wonders."

Both are a part of the prayer of quiet. To reach either you need to pass through noisy regions of the mind to remote inner zones of stillness, a most difficult journey. Saint Gregory wrote: "He who struggles inwardly must practice, at every moment, these four actions: humility, extreme attention, resistance to outward thoughts, and prayer."

On several occasions I went to the Abbey of Gethsemani, in Kentucky, to give lectures and tried living the life of a Trappist for a few days. That was more difficult than the life I lived as a military man during the Second World War and in the Korean conflict. As someone said of contemplative religious: "They are in a state of intense inner activity and a highly mobilized attention."

A nun once told me that she hesitates to take long walks at her convent because it causes others to say, "I wish I didn't have anything more to do than that." For all they know she may have learned the prayer of quiet. I have often thought that it would be a good idea if you walked ten miles for every book read so that the material would have a chance to become a part of you. Information without realization—that's a danger in the realm of the spirit.

The spiritual search needs some simplification of life, a certain asceticism. That is the price you pay. If you want to be "collected" inside, you aim at concentration and attention. For this, peace, beauty and a slow tempo are the surroundings most helpful.

With age you should begin to see that the less you push for personal advantage the better chance you have to know freedom, something not outside yourself but within. Many people make a great to-do over their rights and their freedoms, but miss finding the things they talk about, no matter how many laws they break or how many governments they overthrow. Those mobs filling the newscasts on television, with chants and clenched fists, how many will be free inside themselves?

Edith Hamilton observed that freedom was born in ancient Greece because "there men limited their own freedom." The Greeks believed that limits are good and were appalled by extremes, avoiding excesses to keep a firmer hold on reality.

It is possible also to do poorly in spirit even while keeping all laws of the land. Thucydides makes Pericles speak of "the unwritten laws whose transgression brings shame." Pericles even implied that unwritten laws are more important than written. Miss Hamilton, in discussing those benign attitudes, said that the Athenian accepted as the basic condition of freedom "obedience to kindness and compassion and all the long list of qualities without which life would be intolerable." She felt, as did the Greeks, that limits established by law should be as nothing compared to limits established by a man's free choice. One great legacy the Greeks left us is "the idea that only the man who holds himself within self-chosen limits can be free."

Although nobody can be wholly unselfish, by old age one should realize that most troubles spring from selfishness—war, energy shortages, fanaticism, pollution, auto accidents, crime. Sadness usually arises from some excessive concern for self.

Illness sometimes exists in the realm of selfishness. A truly sick person is one thing, but an imaginary invalid needs be filed under affliction of the spirit rather than of the body. Some people see advantages in illness—a chance for attention, a chance to get even, a recompense for guilt. They cherish a miserable *modus vivandi*. A perverse need for sickness leads to a dramatization of it. When illness is imaginary the will to get better might be weak and no medicine cures it. The flaw is profitable for pharmaceutical companies, if for nobody else.

What happens to the spirit when the mind goes completely out of focus and stays that way? I don't know. We have all seen those apparently finished lives, still ignored by death, filed away. Even to recall such takes courage. To be spared senility, that inverted childhood, is a prayer worth praying. To be helplessly old as once we were helplessly young, "O Lord, deliver us!"

As for lesser handicaps, they might spur some special achievement. I knew a man born with a withered hand and a defective leg who became brilliant in table tennis and billiards. So in old age a decline of the outer self may spur an achievement of the inner self. The law of compensation, I believe it is called.

If you have developed any kind of inner life, the years after retirement will require more than trivial pursuits. In our culture everyone is apt to be at the mercy of the trivial; avoiding it won't be easy.

To avoid trivialities, as the outward life narrows and you awaken "the other life" within, an interest in the arts can be most helpful. This may mean making a fresh start because in our school days the arts were usually neglected. The word art, as I recall, was seldom mentioned outside of philosophy classes in which we talked at length about art being the good, the true, and the beautiful. But we could not recognize a work of art if confronted with it. We talked so much about it that we began to think of it as philosophy, something it surely is not.

We got the impression that only intellect gets at truth. We did not realize that the intuitions of artists may reveal truth in a way that the intellect alone cannot. With certain subtleties art communicates to the consciousness truth not knowable in any other way. There is a danger of giving so much stress to the intellect that the intuitions are lost for lack of use, or mistrust, or because you feel guilty about them.

Common sense comes from a wonderful balance between reason and intuition. In that balance, where good judgment thrives, there is sentiment without sentimentality, realism without despond.

T. S. Eliot, aware of spiritual possibilities, said: "It

is ultimately the function of art, in imposing a credible order upon ordinary reality, and thereby eliciting some perception of an order *in* reality, to bring us to a condition of serenity, stillness and reconciliation."

There is nothing like a vision of order to bring the spirit alive. Walter Kerr wrote in *The Decline of Pleasure:* "It has always fascinated me to watch people coming out of theaters. When they have not enjoyed themselves they seem tired and they want to go home. When they have enjoyed themselves, it is as clear from their muscle tone as it is from their eyes: They are alive and they are ready for something, whatever that something may be. The difference is as simple and as literal as that. A vision of order wakes everyman up."

Since the arts show man's vision of order and the sciences explore God's, the two together help sensitize the spirit to the glories of reality. Bernard Berenson said that through art he grew to see the wonders of nature; it was a helpful step, he said, to move from understanding the relatively simple man-made designs to the more remarkable designs of the Almighty.

So old people, with a new-found leisure, might use the arts and sciences to sensitize their souls to a world the Creator has made. This might be a high form of worship. The most pleasing thing you can do for a human artist is to admire his work, and so standing in awe of creation would seem to be prayer of a high order.

Every concern of yours, whether for arts and sciences or anything else, has something to do with what you become. Life, in time, distills you to an essence. What is the sediment like at the bottom of the cup: bitter, benign, boorish, beautiful? Do you live with a purpose? Does what you do have meaning and somehow fit into the framework of the world? Have you enough strength of character to make old age a positive time?

The distillation gives the answers. It reveals what you have experienced and what you have become. And if you have become *somebody*, your soul will sing.

18

Strictly Personal

A Persian fairy tale tells of three princes from the land called Serendip—later known as Ceylon and now as Sri Lanka—who traveled about the world seeking treasure. They failed to find exactly what they sought, but discovered things that were even better. From this comes the word serendipity.

In my life when I get what I aim for it is not so remarkable as what comes seemingly by chance. Such a fortuitous happening, in Christian writings, is called the providential. The search, though, is necessary, for the usual thing happens while making some effort and not while sitting around waiting.

How little one foresees! If at age twenty a Voice from on High had directed me to write my life's script, the following years would have been less interesting. I had small expectations. Things that have happened were at that time beyond my imagination or willingness to request. I became aware of this while writing an autobiography, *Notre Dame Remembered*.

At twenty I may have decided that all my years should be spent in daily journalism. Although in youth I enjoyed being a newspaperman it is not the kind of work in which I could grow old. Never would I have put into my script the Second World War and the Korean conflict.

Once in the service I would not have thought to assign myself to riding herd on war correspondents or living in a deserted Buddhist monastery writing the military history of what had gone on in India, Burma, China, and Ceylon. As for the role of university professor I would not have dared request it. At twenty how could I have decided that I should spend the first decade of retirement writing books set in Fiji, Japan, Korea, Burma, China, and the Philippines. All such were beyond my dreams. Providential assignments are so superior to our own small expectations.

Youth is unaware that the things nearest the heart, at the time, may not always stay there. We change. On his eighty-fifth birthday Fred Astaire said that he does not miss dancing, and had someone predicted that twenty years earlier, he would not have believed it. Pierre Teilhard de Chardin, after giving much of his life to paleontology, said near the end, "I am now experiencing a kind of nausea for fossils. Explain that to me if you can!"

In my own life the years as film critic seem more remote than do those of childhood on the farm. In his autobiography Graham Greene said of his years as a critic: "How, I find myself wondering, could I possibly have written all those film reviews?"

Perhaps the answer is in Boswell's *Life of Johnson*. Goldsmith says, "I think, Dr. Johnson, you don't go to the theatre now. You give yourself no more concern about a new play than if you had never had anything to do with the stage." Johnson replies, "But as we advance in the journey of life we drop some of the things that have pleased us; whether it be that we are fatigued and don't choose to carry so many things any further, or that we find other things that we like better."

Jung also observed, as mentioned earlier, that some attitudes appropriate to life's morning are inappropriate in the afternoon. A striving toward material things comes natural to the young, he said, but in an old person is "a neurotic hindrance." In early life one tries to come to terms with the outer world, but later that effort should be directed toward the inner self, bringing a new power that comes with renewal.

A change in life requires some courage. In taking early retirement from the classroom to give full-time to writing, I knew I was moving into a chancy line of trade— the finished product may be unacceptable. And I was warned that Social Security and retirement payments would be forever twenty percent less than if I waited until age sixty-five.

I also knew that writing is harder than teaching; it requires more self-discipline. In teaching, some disciplines are applied from without: I never cut a class because students would be sitting there waiting, and I never entered the classroom unprepared because I did not want to look silly. But in writing the discipline must come from within. This morning no one cares whether or not I put words on paper; it would be easy to promise myself that I will get around to it tomorrow. Freedom is hard to handle.

I left teaching because I felt the inner nudge. As Malcom Muggeridge said, the important things in life, the ones that really matter, are thrust upon us. They do not come after weighing matters pro and con. Such choices are for the uncommitted. "An inner momentum carries one along," wrote Muggeridge. "Each step seems, at the same time, both adventitious and inevitable. It is a kind of sleep-walking."

Of this, too, I was aware while writing the autobiography. In reviewing my life I saw things fit together and realized that deep down inside there is a "master form" that does not give way to experiences but holds firm all the way.

The vision of a remarkable whole gets lost because we recall experiences at random. Living can be similar to attending a wonderful play and sleeping through some of the best parts. That is unfortunate, because if you don't see life adding up, you find it inane. In seeing the shape of your life you give it an importance not evident when seen as bits and pieces. Fragments of experience, minor at the time, take on meaning when part of a pattern, as tesserae gain in importance when part of a mural.

In seeing things fit together you give back to the world some of its lost sense of unity. You need not proclaim this from the rooftop; just being aware is enough. It will rub off. Maybe religion brings that inner need to fit everything together into a whole.

The more we "see" the more we become. A deeper vision develops a more complete human being. Any increased awakening throws some light into that darkness which falls so readily across the spirit. If for no other reason increased consciousness is worth developing for its civilizing effect. The most cohesive vision is defective because human beings are defective, and yet an approximate unity is worth creating because it is better than standing there feeling overwhelmed by chaos.

That is why I often urge old people to write the story of their lives. As I said earlier these make wonderful heirlooms, but, even more important, the manuscripts help the writers see how providence has shaped their lives, causing them to say, "And to think I hardly noticed!"

We don't cherish until late in life such things as old diaries, old photographs, old letters, and old experiences. At eighty a farmer in England spoke of a chair his father had made, something he failed to cherish until too late: "I would love to know where that chair is this minute, that I would! I would know it no sooner I see it. Silly fool, I gave it away! Pity. The chair Father made. I see him makin' it an' I give it away!"

In approaching age sixty, Mary and I toyed with the idea of retiring in Europe. While walking toward the Notre Dame dining hall one morning in November of 1970, the thought struck me to write a book about why Americans retire abroad. The nudge was so definite that before the morning was out I had booked a flight to Europe for the Christmas holidays.

Mary went with me on some of the trips to Portugal, Spain, Ireland, England, Italy and Greece. While she gathered material in American embassies, questioned real estate agents, and checked the cost of things, I sought out retired Americans for interviews.

The first interview was with a small gray-haired artist, effervescent for seventy. She grew up in Seattle but had lived in Portugal for thirty years. Her home was near Sintra, a resort for the rich and the royal; her living room window framed a castle of many turrets, straight out of Disney.

"I have noticed," she said, "that Americans have turned their backs on their country in the past couple of years. They used to be attracted here by low-cost living and benign weather, but now they come for reasons of the spirit. They are fleeing something."

The more she spoke, the more I wondered if elderly Americans, like the sailors of Odysseus, did not taste of the lotus and lose their love of home. I knew from the Social Security people that more than 300,000 retired United States citizens were living overseas. I asked, "Why should they pull up roots so late in life and try to transplant them in foreign soil?"

The elderly artist said that the main reason was disillusionment. In the late 1960s when campuses seethed and cities burned, they needed to escape. The old neighborhood was no longer safe.

At the time we began our research, in the early 1970s, the CBS program, *60 Minutes*, compared crime in New York City with that in London, two cities of similar size. Mike Wallace reported that in the past year there had been 1,117 murders in New York City and only 51 in all of Greater London.

Bad conditions at home came up again during an interview in Ireland with an attorney from Washington, D.C. He and his wife had first visited Ireland in April of 1969, more out of curiosity than anything else, and returned five times in two years. They liked what they saw.

"Nobody here tries to oversell us," he said. "Nobody tries to shortchange us. For instance, we noticed that in the village churches there aren't any locks on the poor box. Here people respect the rights of others.

"We contrasted what we found here with what is happening in Washington where personal property has lost all rights. The thing that really made us determined to come and live here was when 25,000 people came to Washington saying they were going to stop the government from operating. That was the day that did it!

"We bought a deserted coast guard station at Ardmore, near Cork. We are renovating it for ourselves."

In Portugal, down in the Algarve, a woman from New York spoke much in the same way: "You might say I like it here because things back home were becoming so bad. When you can't walk down the street without fear, and when you know your house is apt to be broken into, it does things to you that are not good. You stop trusting people."

The generation gap of the late 1960s sent some Italian-Americans back to the villages of their birth. The old people were bitter, saying that their children did not respect the old ways, the traditions. They felt they had failed in life because they had not succeeded in passing along their culture. Upon returning to Italy, they were delighted to rediscover their culture in their cousins, even in their nieces and nephews. As one of them said, "Now we feel liberated. Now we can smile again."

Sentiment caused some people to retire abroad. Sometimes it was even sentimentality, a misguided sentiment. Often the retiree had been born in Europe, had come to America in youth, and now had returned to the village to die, a sentimental gesture.

Some of the retirees born in America were also being sentimental. They had worked in Europe in their prime—with the military, business, government, or academia—and were trying to recapture a bright memory. Some could not go home again.

"Quite a few American artists retire here," said Bruno Scarfi at the American embassy in Rome. "By artists I mean not just painters, but poets, musicians, writers and journalists. It is hard for them after living with congenial spirits over here to return to the States.

"It is difficult for them to say at sixty-five, 'Now I am retired.' They still feel the creative drive. Many of them were brilliant in youth and in maturity.

"To watch businessmen retire is usually not so sad because most of them are glad to; that's what they have been working toward. But to watch an artist's powers dwindle, that is sad.

"Usually you will find them renting a room from an old spinster or an old widow. Most never had strong family ties—or weren't capable of keeping them. It is best that they stay here."

The search for a good climate was another reason some Americans gave for leaving home. When I pointed out that Florida and Southern California have better weather than anything Europe can offer, they answered that those two states have become crowded. The Costa del Sol in Southern Spain and the Algarve in Southern Portugal seem more attractive—except that now they, too, are getting crowded.

Money sometimes played a part in the decision to retire abroad. A dollar went a long way when it had top value and living in Europe was cheap. That was changing fast, though, by the time we began our research. Some people may have been less than truthful when they gave the low cost of living as their primary reason for living abroad. Such an explanation came easier than an admission that they were trying to flee something—their children, a bad marriage, the home town. Some were even trying to flee from themselves. They thought that by leaving their country they could take leave of their own flaws. In searching for an unsullied Eden they forgot that the unpleasant facts of the world we have in common will still keep intruding.

A defiance of old age had a place in some Americans' decision. They were out to prove something, making it clear to themselves and to others that they can still do things that take courage. Still live larger than life. The last fling!

For every American who thought retirement in Europe was a good idea there was at least one who was not so sure. I especially remember two in Greece for whom it worked and two in Italy for whom it did not.

An old man in the Greek village of Skepasto said: "I have everything. I grow some of my food. I make my own wine." A retired business executive in Portaria, a village on Mount Pelion, said "What do I lack here? I have my books, my records. Peace. Quiet. A beautiful garden. Pure air and a view of 300 degrees."

It did not work for two elderly women, cousins, who had returned to their birthplace in Italy to find it much changed. A Communist mayor was in charge of a village where the parish priest used to run things. Relatives and friends had either died or moved away. One of the women said, "So we are going back to our old comforts—the refrigerator and the washing machine." One returned to Baltimore and the other to some place in New Jersey.

The world has turned around many times since my book *Why Americans Retire Abroad* came out in 1973. The jacket showed the Statue of Liberty from the back, as the artist in Sintra suggested. That symbol, however, is no longer valid; elderly Americans have slowed their exodus. Maybe their country has improved since those hectic days of unrest, and maybe European countries have declined.

Just to show how things have changed, when I was finishing the book manuscript, television shows and magazine articles began telling how delighted retired Americans are with Poland. Things are plentiful and cheap! I felt guilty for not having included that country. Yet within a few years the television evening news was presenting dreary lines of Poles waiting to get scant supplies. Even Detroit was sending relief packages to Warsaw.

In 1980 a priest in Dublin said to me, "Professor, in the past ten years Ireland has lost its soul." He was referring to materialism that seeped into the crevices of the soul, and, of course, spoiled tranquility as it always does. Retired Americans must have noticed it, too, for their number has declined during the past five years until now there are 6,378 of them in Ireland—not a great decline, but the number has stopped growing.

My colleague, Professor Ronald Weber, was saddened by the changes he found lately in Portugal. He taught there in the 1968–1969 school year and remembered it as a place beautifully kept where one enjoyed civilized service. Upon returning later he found graffiti galore, slovenly service, and things generally run down. Yet Portugal still has 6,624 retired Americans, as large a number as ever; maybe because it is the cheapest place to live in Europe.

The number of American elderly in the United Kingdom has declined; now there are only 12,276 receiving Social Security checks from Washington. The numbers in Greece have declined to 16,780, in Italy to 40,378 and in Spain to 6,068.

Some still try the experiment. For them I advise something that every person I interviewed agreed on: Don't pull up roots until after a trial at living abroad.

A retired executive on Costa del Sol in Spain expressed the unanimous opinion: "Don't sell at home and don't buy here until you have come over and looked at the place. And when you come, don't visit as a tourist. Stay at least three months; six months would be better. Rent a place; don't stay in a hotel. Shop at the market. See how you get along with the maids. Live the life of the place to see if it suits you."

By the time my book was published, Mary and I no longer considered retiring abroad. If roots go deep, we had learned, you had better not rip them up. Cherish them if they bring a consoling sense of things settled down deeply and tranquilly. Unless your past is exceedingly painful, do not go out of your way to disassociate yourself from it.

We believe that if you have accumulated layers of memories in a certain area, you might best live out your days there. Once you develop a feeling of "place" avoid tampering with it, for milieu is more important in age than it was in youth; you depend on it more as adaptability eludes you. You might not have much power in old age, yet you can have influence, which is better, but you can't have it amid the alien corn. So make your last-ditch stand on familiar ground.

About the time the manuscript for *Why Americans Retire Abroad* was completed, in the summer of 1973, I told Professor Ronald Weber, chairman of the department, that I planned to take an early retirement. There was this felt need to give full-time to writing, the inward push that I am always talking about. And besides my zest for teaching had waned during the days of student incivility and did not give promise of returning. The department had three years to find a replacement.

Three years later Professor Elizabeth Christman agreed to join the faculty full-time. For five years she had been teaching in the summer sessions.

Her career, most unusual, might give inspiration to anyone seeking a change of direction in mid-life. She had been with the Harold Ober Literary Agency, in New York, for two decades when at age fifty she decided she wanted to join a university faculty. With only a bachelor's degree she began studying—not missing a day of work—until she had a doctorate from New York University.

In 1969 she joined the Department of English at DePauw University, at Greencastle, Indiana. After age sixty she began writing novels and within six years three were published: *A Nice Italian Girl* (made into a motion picture, *Black Market Baby*), *Flesh and Spirit*, and *A Broken Family*.

The day I decided to take an early retirement to give full-time to writing I did not foresee the unusual direction life would take for me and for Mary. This began when a stranger, a gentleman from Minneapolis, made a telephone call to my home on Saturday morning, April 6, 1974. Would I have breakfast with him in the dining room of the Morris Inn on the Notre Dame campus? He wanted to tell me "about an archbishop in Korea."

For a half hour my host spoke of his friend Harold Henry, a Minnesotan, who had gone to Korea as a missionary at age twenty-four and now, forty years later, had experienced a life of high adventure and remarkable achievement.

"Would that make a good book?" my host asked.

"A very good book."

"Will you write it?"

"Yes," I said instantly. But I immediately began wondering why I should take leave of a Notre Dame classroom to face the rigors of research, travel, and writing. Besides I didn't know Harold Henry and knew little of Korea. And supposing after all of that trouble no publisher would be interested.

Trying to back out I asked my host why he had decided on me. His daughter, he said, had given him a Christmas gift, my book, *Why Americans Retire Abroad*. He had delayed reading it until on spring holiday in Florida, and then he kept saying to himself that the man who wrote this should tell the story of Harold Henry.

I said that I could see no relationship between an archbishop in Korea and elderly Americans retired abroad. My host admitted that neither could he, but that the thought had so haunted him that he had stopped at Notre Dame on the way home to talk with me.

There was no doubt that the idea "felt right" to him and also felt that way to me. Long ago I learned that when that feeling comes you had better respond or else you will regret it later.

I made one last effort to back out. "Suppose the archbishop and I don't get along together?"

"He will come to the College of Saint Thomas next month to receive an honorary degree. At that time he can come to Notre Dame and the two of you can decide whether or not you get along."

Archbishop Henry had hardly landed at the South Bend airport when both of us knew we would enjoy each other's company. That night he told Mary and me fascinating stories and the next morning I put him on a plane for his return to Korea.

That night I took an Aer Lingus flight to Dublin to begin research. Since Harold Henry was a member of Saint Columban's Foreign Mission Society I needed to spend time in the society's world headquarters in Killiney, just south of Dublin on the Irish Sea. After several weeks of research in the archives I brought my notes to Notre Dame to absorb them. Before leaving for Korea I visited Harold Henry's friends in Omaha, Tucson, and El Paso. For six weeks I lived in the archbishop's residence on Cheju Island, off the southern coast of Korea. Later he and I went to Ireland to finish the manuscript. He liked what he read, but died before *Light in the Far East* was published in the fall of 1976.

Although the gentleman from Minneapolis thought only of one book, as did I, that one became the first of a series of seven. Each time I finished a manuscript something unusual came along to nudge me to the next, so that between my sixtieth and seventieth birthdays I also wrote *Mindanao Mission, Fiji Revisited, Japan Journey, Mission in Burma, Maybe a Second Spring* (China) and *Journeys Not Regretted,* the latter about my experiences while writing the other six books.

Because I agreed to tell Archbishop Henry's story, Mary's life also changed direction in a dramatic way. On the night of Thursday, May 23, 1974 when I was flying to Ireland to begin research, I got to thinking that with this trip to the archives I was finally committing myself to write the archbishop's biography. No turning back now.

That night my friend, Father Anthony Lauck, C.S.C., was retiring from the Notre Dame art department and his colleagues were honoring him with a dinner, one I had planned on attending. Knowing that I was out over the Atlantic, my friend Professor Thomas Stritch asked Mary if she would care to take my place at the dinner. There she met Father Louis Putz, C.S.C., recently retired from the faculty. He asked her what she planned on doing the next morning.

"I'm playing golf," she replied.

"Could you postpone the game?"

The next morning Father Putz told Mary that he was going to start the Forever Learning Institute, a school for anyone fifty-five years of age or older. He had access to the old Bendix mansion and felt that retired Notre Dame professors would volunteer as teachers. Would she help him? He needed publicity.

Within a few days Mary was visiting newspaper offices and radio and television stations in the South Bend area handing out announcements about the new school for older adults scheduled to open in the fall of 1974. At one television station a producer invited her to go on the air to tell the story. After she did just that, he invited her to return for more of the same. In time she was producer and hostess of *The Mary Fischer Show*. At age sixty she was getting her own television program.

Mary had been a leader in volunteer work for years. The day that our youngest child started school, in 1956, she went to the children's hospital, down the street, and volunteered to work with crippled children in the exercise pool. About the same time she began volunteer work at Saint Joseph's Hospital a few blocks in the other direction.

When the Snite Museum of Art opened at Notre Dame, in 1980, she volunteered as a staff assistant and went through a year of demanding study in art history before starting to give gallery tours. She does similar work in the South Bend Art Center and at the Northern Indiana Historical Museum. Mary is also a member of numerous boards such as the Friends of the Notre Dame Library and the Friends of the Snite. She is still involved in all of these things, plus others too numerous to list.

For years Mary has said, "The greatest luxury in life is to be able to do something for nothing." When Hugh Downs was host of the national television show, *Over*

Easy, the producer of the show heard this about Mary. He sent a writer and a director from California to prepare a script about her, and ten days later a film crew flew in from the coast to start shooting the documentary.

The opening scene is a close-up of the golden dome atop Notre Dame's administration building. The camera tilts downward showing Mary coming out the front door, descending the steps, and placing books into the basket of her bike.

It was a fitting opening because Mary has taken many courses at Notre Dame: modern drama, Milton, Shakespeare, tax law, to name a few. Her course in gerontology has had an influence on both our lives; it got us interested in problems of growing old—that plus our own accumulation of years—so that her television show and much of my writing have sprung from that interest.

Mary receives quite a bit of mail. She feels letters should be acknowledged within twenty-four hours, and so she sometimes arises at four in the morning to answer them. Her pace continues for another twelve hours. She works longer and harder without pay than many people do for pay.

What am I doing? Shortly before eight, six days a week, I walk the mile to the Notre Dame library, where in room G-26 I feed a blank sheet of paper into the typewriter and hope for the best. The day I completed the autobiography I started this book, and, with the permission of God, I will start another the day this one is finished.

At noon, as mentioned earlier, I usually walk the mile and a half to the dining room at Saint Mary's College. After lunch I spend an hour reading in the lovely new college library, before returning to my office. Since writing in the afternoon rarely goes well I am apt to walk home at about three o'clock.

Mary and I have not regretted spending our years of retirement in the house on Saint Vincent Street which we bought when joining the Notre Dame faculty in 1947. Many mornings while walking up the tree-lined avenue, with the golden dome glinting just ahead, I recall something a young secretary said nearly forty years ago. She had quit her job at the university, but after a year returned to it. I asked where she had been and she said, "I took a job with an industry in South Bend; it paid better but I always felt homesick. This is such a nice place to come to the first thing each morning."

19

How We Feel about Old Age

Mary and I were married on April 10, 1939. In the ensuing years neither has used the other as a crutch. We developed our own talents and interests, and at the same time grew closer in ways of looking at life and in values, both moral and aesthetic. For instance, the marriage would have been strained had one approved of abortion while the other disapproved, and if one was for honest dealing and the other for wheeling-dealing, and what if one played acid rock and leafed through comic books while the other preferred Bach and read the classics? Values, moral and aesthetic, ought to be somewhat similar.

We both, for example, have approaches to death that are nearly identical. My attitude toward it began forming at age seven while walking in a field brown with autumn. With a stick I flipped over a dead squirrel and was shocked by a seething multitude of maggots. Such a vision is still with me the evenings I walk among the stones of old friends in Cedar Grove Cemetery, at the edge of the Notre Dame campus. Since that experience at seven, I have wondered why people are solicitous over where or how they are buried. Why fret over the plot of ground, the kind of coffin, and the view from the site? On television a funeral director showed a coffin with a velvet interior and an "adjustable mattress."

Although Mary and I care about life neither wants to live so long that the days begin to lack definition. Already aware of the nuances of approaching destruction, we wonder how the end will come. We do not fear death itself but greatly dread a prolonged agony of dying. To be kept alive by gadgets is dehumanizing, and since that is the direction medicine has taken, we envy those who go swiftly into that good night.

In such fear we are not alone, said a television documentary, *Growing Old in America*. It began with Hugh Downs, the host, saying that at the start of this century life expectancy was forty-seven and now it is seventy-four, as we hurry toward the Era of the Truly Old. Although we live longer than our ancestors, he said, and in most cases live better, it is not all to the good: "A specter hangs over old age greater than the fear of death itself. It's the fear of disability and loss of independence."

On the screen patients were sprawled in their beds penetrated by plastic tubes and hemmed in by tanks, monitors and bottles—the ganglia of high-tech medicine. Many of the comatose were being kept alive at a cost of $600 a day while their families went bankrupt prolonging a hopeless case.

Technology is an enemy when it extends existence in a dehumanizing way. Out of fear that their final days may be completely lacking in dignity, more than eighty percent of the old people interviewed said that they do not want gadgets to keep them existing. Their preferences, though, get all entangled in moral and legal issues.

Doctors admit that the fear of lawsuits causes them to do unreasonable things. They call it "aggressive treatment," words that bring a shudder to the soul.

After seeing *Growing Old in America* even the young must have felt uneasy. The three-hour documentary ended with a young man saying, "The old are us— it's our future selves—you and me."

Wishing for death and fearing it are both flaws. Since the coming of death is as natural, and as inevitable, as the setting of the sun, it is best accepted that way. Death is less of an ogre when you admit that it fits into the scheme of things; it is as much a part of life as is breathing. Billions have known the experience and billions more will know it.

When a friend died, Teilhard de Chardin spoke of him as ending "with simplicity and style." In later years Teilhard prayed "to end well," and wrote to a friend, "Pray for me to the Lord, that He may allow me to 'keep in form.'" He had a reverence for death and not a gloomy anxiety, just as in the *Upanishads* a husband said to his wife: "As a lump of salt, when thrown into the sea, melts away and the lump cannot be taken out, even so, O Mailreyi, is the individual 'self' dissolved in the Eternal."

Another problem that often faces the elderly is whether they should live alone or live with somebody. A British film, *The Whisperers*, confronted this dilemma.

An old lady, played by Dame Edith Evans, is pained by the friction of abrasive years. She lives alone in a flat that exudes a damp, penitential air. Her lawless son returns home just long enough to hide stolen money in the flat, and because of this she is robbed and beaten.

The welfare people think it would be best if her husband, who had deserted her years ago, were to return to live with her. He does return, but it is evident from the start that it would be better if he had not. He leaves shortly.

The old lady returns to her empty flat and smiles at the drip-drip of a leaking faucet. It is an old friend. Suddenly the audience is struck with the realization that it is better to live surrounded by friendly inanimate objects than to live among incompatible human beings.

Whether or not to live alone? There is no simple answer. Only after looking carefully at the individual and at the circumstances can one make a good guess. Some people enjoy aloneness, but others will live with almost anyone rather than face an empty room. Hell may be "other people," the theme of Sartre's *No Exit*, but for some people "no people" is even more hell.

Parents sometimes act like children and begin looking to their own children for support, nourishment, and care of all sorts. In senescence the selfishness of infancy may come surging back. This return to second childhood is an immaturity that was there all along, becoming more dramatic in time. With enough strength of character you might ward off a second childhood, but there are no guarantees.

In a poll, nine out of ten aging parents said they prefer *not* to live with their children. The National Association of Health observed that old people stay younger and more truly alive in their own homes than elsewhere. If people do live with others it is best to pay attention to Kahlil Gibran: "But let there be spaces in your togetherness. For the pillars of the temple stand apart. And the oak tree and the cypress grow not in each other's shadow."

In stepping down the rungs of the ladder it is better to lower expectations than to revolt; revolting leads to "second adolescence," a more usual problem than second childhood. The elderly adolescent, like the young, swings to extremes, lacking consistency and taking a know-it-all attitude. The problem is of two extremes, self-assertion or over-dependence. While there is no defense against second childhood if something goes awry in the brain, second adolescence might well be avoided if you admit it can happen and feel a great desire not to let it.

Whether or not to wait for death in a nursing home is another dilemma that faces the disabled and their relatives. This decision is difficult because, as Bernard Baruch observed at ninety, the most prized possession in old age is independence. There are exceptions: some old people seem to relish being dependent and in making unnecessary demands on others.

I don't agree with the generalization that it is unfortunate that old people are sent to nursing homes. I would prefer such if unable to care for myself. I could feel more at ease if my burden rests on someone whose vocation it is to care for the infirm. It is a matter of not wanting to stunt somebody else's life.

Mind you, I do not see retirement homes and nursing homes as aspects of Eden. My great hope is that I will be graced with the attitude shown by the woman in a nursing home who wrote: "So it was rough. And sometimes it was sweet. But I have lived to be ninety-three. And that's wonderful."

Such attitude does not always prevail; those small rooms can hold a tremendous lot of loneliness. Mutual senescence does not draw people together. Life can become so dreary that old people feel as did Mephistopheles in Goethe's *Faust:* Everything that exists deserves to be reduced to nothingness. Such dejection leads to what Hemingway called "the tyranny of the weak."

Loneliness arrives even before one enters a retirement home or a nursing home. A physician said that he thought ninety-nine percent of his patients were lonely people. Many of them were retreating into a self-imposed loneliness upon finding the experiences of life too painful. At the root of all addictions, for example, is a painful knot of loneliness.

A photographer for the Louisville *Courier-Journal* won a national award for a photo of lonely people. The picture, taken at the busiest intersection in town, shows the look on the faces of a dozen pedestrians waiting for the light to change. If you want to see that look, ride a subway and study the faces of people sitting opposite you.

Loneliness is not aloneness—not solitude. It is an ominous burden, an empty brooding that weighs one down even in crowded places—especially in crowded places.

Those who are lonely in retirement were probably that way before retirement, only then the blur of making a living distracted them from the full force of pain. If distraction is a part of treatment, the best one is something that brings satisfaction. Creative people find this to be true. A psychoanalyst said: "The artist is a successful neurotic, who conquers his loneliness through the creative process." Leonardo da Vinci must have sensed that when he observed, "When you are all alone, you are all your own."

As long as there is consciousness, it is a great grace to continue catching the spectacular beauty of the present moment. As someone said, should the moon and the stars appear only once in a century how thrilling it would be to see them. Unawareness is a waste of life; the unfocused life is something to dread. Not to do things with attention turns existence into a blur.

John Burroughs, with the grace of attention in old age, said: "I still find each day too short for all the thoughts I want to think, all the walks I want to take, all the books I want to read, all the friends I want to see. The longer I live the more my mind dwells upon the beauty and the wonder of the world." And it is said of Plotinus, the philosopher, that "he retained the feeling that he was living amongst mysteries and miracles until the end of his days." Burroughs and Plotinus must have had a strong sense of themselves as a part of creation; such awareness may be at the heart of real spirituality.

It is not enough in old age to enjoy the fruits of your experiences; you ought to keep collecting them. The effort, of course, will be less outward and more inward as time goes by.

Reading, as a way of gaining new experience, grows in importance for Mary and me. All of our lives we have haunted libraries and now books mean more to us than ever. Our approach has changed some: we look more for formation than for information. An encyclopedia informs, but does little to form you, while a wise book or a work of art both inform and form, making one more complete.

Books can help, through the years, to develop a point of view. I don't mean an opinion about the United Nations, or income tax, or social security, but an ingrained philosophy that does not shift with the fads of this unsettled age. Your settled attitude needs to ride like a seaworthy ship through the mental chaos that is especially threatening with the rise of the mass media. In your point of view you will see some things as good, some as evil, and most as a blending. Then maybe you will find peace and satisfaction in your inner world in spite of the evening news.

"The sole advantage in possessing great works of literature," said George Santayana, "lies in what they can help us to become." That is the sole advantage of any art. If a masterpiece were in the jungle, covered with vines and forever hidden from human eyes, it might just as well not exist. It can only lift life by reaching human beings. I do not believe in art for the sake of art but for the sake of humanity.

When we become more demanding of how time is used, it is harder for us to find books that delight. Most fall into one of three categories: style without content, content without style, and neither style nor content.

A French priest, Pere Auguste Valensin, S.J., wrote in his journal about how much he must grapple with a thought to explain it in a way that will spare others the struggle. He concluded: "That is the secret of my clarity.

I pay dearly for it." The authors I read must have paid the price.

Each year I find increased enjoyment in making contact with an interesting mind. Unless a discerning and lively personality is evident within a few paragraphs, the book goes back on the shelf.

The better the piece of writing the longer it takes me to get through it. For instance, Somerset Maugham's *The Summing Up*—it is not a large book but it took a while to read because each page started flights of speculation. The excitement of an interesting mind causes me to pause often to make notes and think the thoughts stirred up. How much I enjoy a piece of writing can be measured by the number of note cards filled while reading it.

To assimilate what is read is never easy. Time and maturity help the difficult process of restating in your own terms the things heard, seen, experienced. You will have to struggle toward realizations, reaching each as you become ready for it. Fortunately, in old age experience often serves as a magnet to draw meaning from words, meaning that was there all the time but you were not ready for it.

To over-simplify, I might say that in youth I read for amusement, in middle age for information, and in old age to spot the sign-posts near the end of the road. Maybe I am hurrying ahead trying to find out how the story ends. Reading gives some sense of the pattern of life. Scarcely anything happens now that does not bring to mind something in the past. The story keeps repeating. I will end but it will not.

Books may also help one come to terms with things long dreamed about. One learns it is wise not to try to realize some dreams, but just enjoy them. For instance, a man who had long dreamed of the glories of the sea, when finally exposed to the rigors of its storms, decided that for him the sea was best viewed from the comfort of a fireplace with a good volume of adventure in his hand. He finally came to see he was in love with books about adventure, not with adventure itself.

Mary and I travel less these days, but some people do not begin ranging widely until they are our age. An elderly English spinster used to go by buggy to friends within an eight-mile radius of her home; the rest of the world she described "beyond calling distance." Scarcely any place now is beyond calling distance, and that is wonderful so long as travelers realize that a journey is worth the effort if it teaches them to see and hear and understand. If it only kills time, they might as well stay home and play cards.

The experience of travel has value when it causes some unfolding of the inner self. As a child I used to look at a fern each day to see how a tight, tiny knot unfolded little by little into a graceful leaf. The experience of travel brings such an unfolding in some people and leaves others untouched.

Flashes of awareness come not so much from seeing something new but from seeing old things in a new light, from observing everything as it really is, a mystery. A young woman dying in a concentration camp could from her bed catch a glimpse of a chestnut tree. She spoke often of the tree even though only one twig and two blossoms were visible. That scant bit in the window helped her make a spiritual retreat.

Travel at its best is a form of spiritual retreat. Old age is especially ready for meditation in improbable places. Ancient truths that have become commonplace through repetition, hollow phrases lacking in meaning, may suddenly stab you with a realization, if you are touched by the right object. And you never know when it will happen.

When Mary and I were in Lisbon, for instance, the museum of royal coaches did something for our spirits. The coaches stand there, row on row, encrusted in grandeur beyond description, centuries old and once the focus of adulation. They stand now without meaning, except as curiosities, unless we hear them speak the old truths about how fame and fortune, and even greatness, pass away—and how the past is covered with the silt of the present which, in turn, awaits its turn.

The ancient coaches also teach the difference between craftsmanship and technology. They are a display of craftsmanship, just as an auto show is a display of technology. Standing in front of them you find yourself thinking that there must be more satisfaction in craftsmanship than in technology because craft has in it the feeling of the individual. The men who built those coaches would have been insulted if anyone had suggested built-in obsolescence. They had much wisdom in their hands.

I am old-fashioned enough to find something holy in craftsmanship. Something made with care is born of charity. An architect said that a good concept can be spoiled by cheap workmanship. Even small matters such as how moldings fit and how doors swing are important. As he put it, "God is in the details."

In Lisbon we overheard an American girl say something that indicated she had been looking at things of the past long enough to compare them with the present. She was groping for some kind of truth when she said, "It's like we don't have culture, but we are modernized." Just what realization was forming in her mind I am not sure, but she was groping for something. That is what I mean by travel being a form of retreat. If it sharpens awareness, something so easily blunted, new places speak to us with more eloquence than do the familiar ones that we listen to without attention.

In walking around old towns I sometimes realized what Cicero meant when he wrote of "the power of admonition that is in places." Travel has also made me aware of the largeness of the planet, and to think it is just a cinder in the cosmos! Anything that increases awe of creation is good for the spirit.

The place that money deserves in life is another thing Mary and I agree on. Were one of us a spendthrift and the other a miser, life would be awful. We agree that being rich means not needing anything beyond minimum comfort; as the Chinese say, "To be poor and feel rich is better than being rich and feeling poor."

"Thinking about sense-objects will attach you to sense-objects," is a saying from the *Bhagavad Gita*. Attachments start you on a downhill journey because they become addictive, and when the addiction is thwarted you get angry. Anger causes a confused mind, making you forget the lessons of experience, and so you fail to see life's main purpose.

With such awareness, Christian monks and Buddhist monks speak of "detachment." They realize that as long as you cling you will be blinded to the way you ought to go. Epictetus said to avoid grasping anything as though it is yours because it really is not: "While he permits you to possess it, hold it as something not your own, as do travelers at an inn." The philosopher felt you would not be apt to covet anything, if daily you kept death before your eyes.

In old age you have a special need for something that cannot be taken away. Since money might vanish it is not so important as inner strength.

People who keep grabbing possessions and fretting over them are not apt to know "the peace that passes all understanding."

On a radio talk show a man complained to a psychiatrist that he has a buyer's addiction. He goes to every sale and buys things not needed. He cannot resist. The psychiatrist told him that he is trying to fill an inner void. The way to fill it is to do something for somebody else. As a suggestion the psychiatrist advised the addict to offer to do the buying for the housebound; by using his expertise for someone else he might rid himself of his own emptiness.

Grasping shows up in many ways. For example, a visitor went to a Quaker meeting house, one that scarcely anyone had attended for years. While sitting alone with eyes closed he suddenly heard a shuffle and a bearded man said, "Pardon me, this is my seat." He needed to sit on a certain chair even though the hall was nearly deserted. The old man had lived through years of tightly woven days, and now that there was a little more "give" in them he had a chance to become more expansive, but could not bring himself to "let go." He, like everyone, needs to let himself grow a little because there is truth in what an old Irish woman observed: "If you don't get better, you get worse. There is no standing still this side of the grave." She was aware that the winter of life need not also be the winter of the soul.

Greed, which is selfishness, causes more trouble in the world than any other human flaw. It destroys families and friendships, and causes conflicts between nations. What a terrible affliction it is.

To have or to be? That is the question. People who care most about having tend to be grabby, but those who care about being somebody worth being develop their inner selves.

All of this has something to do with temperance. Until I heard a sermon in Westminster Abbey I thought of temperance in limited terms, as the avoidance of alcohol. Temperance, the preacher explained, is the proper use of earthly things—automobiles, television, telephones and all things that are good in themselves but through insensitive use are spoiled.

To *be* more you need to *know* more, not facts, but realizing things with a kind of wisdom that reflects a deep sense of life and an awareness of the spiritual. As the *Vedanta* says, the highest truth is the truth that there exists only One Eternal Being, and that everything is derived from this One. In old age there is a better chance than in youth of realizing such things.

If you grade yourself by accumulations—properties, cars, stocks—you sell yourself short. You gain durable satisfaction only by becoming somebody inside. Jung said: "A sense of wider meaning to one's existence is what raises a man beyond mere getting and spending."

By discovering a wider meaning you will need less and might well find some serenity. Your needs will be fewer when your inner resources become your riches. Somerset Maugham said that although he had a villa by the sea he could give it up and live in one room, asking only to have some simple food and plenty of books from the public library and enough paper and pens for writing.

The mystical poet, Saint John of the Cross, said: "He that knows how to die to all things will have life in all things." The way to keep things from damaging you is to hold them lightly. Winning a million-dollar lottery won't help much if you are a grasping person. An inner life is what you need, not the money.

Success comes from making a contribution to life. Those who ask "How much does it pay?" may in the long run feel hollow compared with those who want to know, "Is it worth doing?"

Mary and I agree that the freedom that comes with retirement brings a special time to do things worth doing. It is sad if an old person, who should know better, kills time—the opposite of finding meaning in life. Were one to throw away money the relatives might discuss institutionalization, but it is possible to throw away time, more valuable than money, and appear normal.

Leisure and sloth are not related. Retired people at loose ends, feeling slothful, become morose. A retired steelworker said with dejection, "All my time is free, but I can't do much with it." Another retired man said, "You take three hours for breakfast and the newspaper. Then you fuss around in the basement and garden. They're building a garage in back of us. I go over and 'supervise' the job. I don't know whether it's leisure or wasted time." Neither man feels he is accomplishing anything.

Through accomplishment you earn the right to be judged as an individual; otherwise you may be lumped into some faceless category such as "senior citizens," or, worse, "golden-agers." But don't complain about being filed in a category; instead earn your individuality by living with courage and discipline.

Lacking accomplishment, you will become frustrated and make a pest of yourself by demanding things. Society allows you only a certain amount of demanding, and once you have used your quota you are scorned. To avoid the backlash, grow old feeling that you have more duties than you have rights.

Without a sense of accomplishment you will live from fix to fix—alcohol, over–the–counter drugs, too much food, a boat, a car, an affair, anything to try to fill the empty space. You need to feel connected to something beyond yourself, or else you suffer an uneasiness of being at loose ends. You may even become allergic to yourself. Some people cannot stand their own company.

Indulging in trivial amusements, one step above vegetation, is not much help. If that is the only way you can avoid the dry rot that comes with apathy, rigidity, and emptiness, so be it, but surely you can do better.

Hobbies help but the trouble is they may become

boring. Sooner or later you need to do something that you think is worthwhile or you start feeling like a parasite. The inane becomes hard to bear. If you want to turn a hobby into your main interest you will need to treat it like a vocation and not a mere divertissement. In your eyes it must have value. You should not, for instance, take up painting, golf, or bridge if those activities seem silly to you. Knitting and gardening are wonderful for some people but not for others. If your new leisure does not bring a new amplitude into life something is missing.

When leisure hours creep slowly by like a train of empty boxcars they are lacking in satisfaction. You need to fill them in such a way that neither you, nor anyone else, would think of applying the word "leisure" to them. You are most admirably retired when no one thinks of you as being retired.

One of the best things about the leisure of retirement, or so I have found, is being aware that there are many things one need no longer bother with. I keep an imaginary list of them, and it is quite long. For instance, upon receiving a notice of any meeting I toss it away without a second glance and add that to my list. So many things have become inconsequential and boring, such as the yammering of politicians and the vapid talk of coaches and sports figures when interviewed on television. Clichés and banalities are more evident after you have been through life's cycles a few times.

For years you may have been so busy with the urgent that you had scant time for the important, but now you have the time. Leisure is important, and unless what you are doing feels that way to you, it is the wrong use of your own new-found time.

Education is a recurring theme when Mary or I talk about what to do in retirement. In old age we get our last chance to complete ourselves; you might say it is the *only* chance, since youth and middle years are times of preparation.

Too bad one is not born old and then enjoy all of life from that rich perspective. In old age more than in youth you are apt to come upon something that lights up the soul. "That's it!" you exclaim as hundreds of hesitations unite into some understanding. Such wonder Plato called "the source of all philosophy." You can pave the way for such insights, but they come in their own good time. Understanding, like grace, cannot be willed, and no one can thrust it on you, but if you remain open it will arrive. Henri Frederic Amiel ended his 14,000-page journal: "It is never too late to be wise."

Schooling makes the unfamiliar familiar, but it takes education to show how glorious is the unfamiliar found within the familiar. We only see such things when we are ready for them. With each passing year we ought to be ready to see more. And yet we are not only deficient at seeing *into* something but are inadequate at seeing the surface of things as well. This was demonstrated at a Congress of Psychology in Germany when a crowd of presumably trained observers were subjected to a surprise experiment. Two men rushed into the hall, one fired a shot, one jumped on top of the other, and then both rushed from the room. Forty psychologists answered sev-

eral questions about the event. Twenty-five percent of
the answers were wrong.

I had a similar experience at Fort Benning during
the Second World War. Thirty officers in an advanced
course were listening to a lecture about observation when
from behind the stands three men rushed forward, things
were yelled, someone fired a shot, a limp figure was
hauled off. Nobody noticed that the one who fired the
shot was the one hauled off.

During moot court, law students at Notre Dame
learn how untrustworthy is human observation. Four
movies have been made of an auto accident, from the four
different corners of an intersection. Four observers are
each shown one film. During the trial they are questioned and often their answers fail to jibe.

If seeing the surface of life is so difficult, how much
more so is seeing the inner life. Yet the effort to see is
needed, else an ill-nourished mind and flaccid spirit
might turn retirement into dreary incarceration.

To see life requires attention. The Japanese say that
even tea should be taken with attention. Thousands of
things deserve it—the leaves in autumn, sunrises, the
whirr of cicadas. If you are alert to creation it will be evident to others, and so in an old body it is still possible to
be the carrier of new life, the life of inspiration. Your attitude in old age is a form of inheritance, something
handed on to those you meet along the road. If you hand
on encouragement of spirit, that will be a more valuable
heirloom than graspable items.

All of this does not have much to do with your IQ.
As Bonhoeffer observed: "There are men of great intel-

lect who are fools, and men of low intellect who are anything but fools." Highly intelligent people can even lack
education.

Someone described educated people as those capable of entertaining others, entertaining new ideas, and
entertaining themselves. If that is true, some people with
high IQs and advanced degrees lack education, for they
are dull indeed. They seem to know so much and understand so little.

Yet there needs to be content in your world if there
is to be contentment. Just as a book devoid of content
lacks interest, so with life. Since meaning is not found in
emptiness, some retired people deteriorate for lack of
content in their lives. Impoverishment of mind might age
one faster than biological decline. One is not really old
until losing inner flexibility, something that can happen
at thirty.

Upon nearing the end of this manuscript, I recall
that Cicero, upon finishing *On Old Age*, said to his friend
Atticus, "I have found writing this book so delightful that
it has not only wiped away all the annoyances of old age
but has rendered it easy and pleasing."

While I would not go that far, I must admit that writing this has done me some good, too. For instance, I am
now nearer the attitude called *wu-shih*, recommended
by the Zen masters. *Wu-shih* means accepting birth,
death and everything between with no fuss. Maybe Zen
pushes this too far, but most people carry fuss too much
the other way.

Now I am also a little closer to understanding the attitude of an old Arab whose tent was pitched next to some

whirling dervishes. Somebody asked him, "How can you stand that commotion? What are you going to do about it?"

He said, "Let 'em whirl."

Writing these pages helped me approach the Greek admonition, "Know thyself," and I better understand the Greek advice, "Nothing to excess."

More than ever I consider that being born is a great gift. To say that life is not worth living shows a lack of gratitude. Yet I must admit that I feel about life the way I do about the Second World War: I am glad to have had the experience, but would not want to go through it again. I am unlike Bernard Berenson who at ninety said: "I would willingly stand at street corners, hat in hand, asking passers-by to drop into it their unused minutes."

If it is true that the human race is still in the making, the next step upward may be mainly spiritual. You can help the species take that step by living an admirable old age. Your own step upward may be infinitesimal, but still it is better than a downward one.